NEGOTIATING RATIONALLY

Max H. Bazerman
Margaret A. Neale

THE FREE PRESS

Copyright © 1992 by Max H. Bazerman and Margaret A. Neale

All rights reserved. No part of this book may be reproduced or trans-
mitted in any form or by any means, electronic or mechanical,
including photocopying, recording, or by any information storage or
retrieval system, without permission in writing from the Publisher.

The Free Press
A Division of Simon & Schuster Inc.
1230 Avenue of the Americas
New York, N.Y. 10020

First Free Press Paperback Edition 1993

Printed in the United States of America

printing number
14 16 18 20 19 17 15

Library of Congress Cataloging-in-Publication Data

Bazerman, Max H.
    Negotiating rationally / Max H. Bazerman, Margaret A. Neale.
        p.   cm.
    Includes bibliographical references and index.
    ISBN 0-02-901986-9
    1. Negotiation.   2. Negotiation in business.   I. Neale, Margaret Ann.
II. Title.
BF637.N4B39   1992
658.4 – dc20   91-34205
                                               CIP

Credits

Grateful acknowledgment is made to the authors and publishers who have granted permission to reprint the following:

Pages 18–19: Illustrations from Max H. Bazerman, *Judgment in Managerial Decision Making,* 84–85. Copyright © 1990 John Wiley & Sons, Inc. Reprinted by permission of John Wiley & Sons, Inc.

Page 25: Auditing problem from Edward J. Joyce and Gary C. Biddle, "Anchoring and Adjustment in Probabilistic Inference," *Journal of Accounting Research* (Spring 1981), 123. Copyright © 1981 University of Chicago Press.

Page 27: Figure 4.1 from G. B. Northcraft and Margaret A. Neale, "Experts, Amateurs, and Real Estate: An Anchoring and Adjustment Perspective on Property Pricing Decisions," *Organizational Behavior and Human Decision Processes* 39 (1987), by permission of Academic Press.

Pages 33–34: Asian disease problem from A. Tversky and D. Kahneman, "The Framing of Decisions and the Psychology of Choice," *Science, 411,* 40 (1981), 453–63. Copyright © 1981 by the American Association for the Advancement of Science.

Page 36: Table 5.1 from D. Kahneman, J. L. Knetsch, and R. Thaler, "Experimental Tests of the Endowment Effect and Coase Theorem," *Journal of Political Economy,* in press. Copyright University of Chicago Press.

Page 51: Figure 7.1 from W. Samuelson and M. H. Bazerman, "Negotiation Under the Winner's Curse," in V. Smith, ed., *Research in Experimental Economics,* vol. 3 (Greenwich, Conn.: JAI Press, 1985).

Page 111: Figure 12.1 from S. Ball, M. H. Bazerman, and J. S. Carroll, "An Evaluation of Learning in the Bilateral Winner's Curse," *Organizational Behavior and Human Decision Processes* 48 (1991), by permission of Academic Press.

To Beta Mannix, Greg Northcraft,
Leigh Thompson, Kathleen Valley, and Sally White,
who have been excellent
colleagues and friends

Contents

PART THREE
Simplifying Complex Negotiations

Preface

Whether you run a corporation, buy a used car, or sometimes disagree with a colleague or your spouse, you need to know how to negotiate. As recently as ten years ago, however, negotiation courses were rarely taught in management schools or executive education programs; now, they're some of the most sought-after courses across the country. At the J.L. Kellogg Graduate School of Management at Northwestern University, negotiation is the most popular course in both our MBA and executive programs. Current and future managers want to know how to get better results in negotiation—they want to know how to negotiate more rationally.

A large number of diverse researchers have studied negotiation, and their work has profoundly affected this book. In addition, we've devoted our own research and teaching over the last decade to helping managers and executives make more rational decisions and attain far stronger outcomes. We've had over ten thousand participants in our programs, and they've helped us understand the changing social and organizational environment they face today and target the problems they must deal with.

We analyzed both how these professionals negotiate rationally and the common reasons why they don't and found amazing consistency in the errors that bright executives make. We've summarized why managers make these errors, and how you can avoid them to become a more rational negotiator—not just while you read the book, but for the rest of your life.

Why is negotiation attracting such attention? Why have negotiation courses become so popular in the last decade? One answer is that recent social and economic changes have made good negotiating skills not just more important, but more difficult to master. Consider the major trends of the past twenty years and how they affect your professional life:

1. *Workforce Mobility.* Unlike past generations, employees these days frequently change jobs. Long-term commitment between employer and employee is rare. White-collar workers often view a job as simply one stepping-stone in an upwardly mobile career; the next step may or may not be with the same organization. These new models of employment require that employees actively negotiate their position in an organization.

2. *Corporate Restructuring.* The 1980s brought on the era of corporate restructuring. Mergers, acquisitions, downsizing, and joint ventures created thousands of new corporate arrangements. Career survival in such an environment depends on good negotiation skills.

3. *Diversified Workforce.* By the year 2000, seventy percent of the entering workforce will be composed of females, minorities, and immigrants. This high diversity will require managers to work with peers, subordinates, and superiors who have very different goals, motivations, and cultural backgrounds. Negotiating sucessfully will be more complex, and good negotiation skills will be critical levers for workplace and workforce productivity.

4. *Service-Sector Economy.* The U.S. has shifted from a manufacturing-based to a service-based economy. Service-sector negotiations are, on average, harder than manufacturing-based negotiations. Buyers and sellers must agree on more ambiguous outcomes. This requires more complex negotiations.

5. *Renegotiation.* The U.S.'s economic decline, and the resulting devastation to organizations affected by it, makes renegotiation more important. When a company is failing, bankruptcy often becomes a more attractive option than fulfilling its obligations to shareholders and/or creditors. Renegotiations also occur between nations, an example being the continual renegotiation of Third World debt.

6. *Global Marketplace.* Twenty years ago, American managers faced a simpler environment. Global competition wasn't a serious threat, and managers could negotiate on their own terms. But, as the industrial leadership of the United States erodes, more and more American managers are negotiating with foreign counterparts who negotiate quite differently than they do.

It seems inevitable that each of these trends will be here for the foreseeable future, making keen negotiation skills a critical tool for the successful executive of the 1990s.

* * *

In the first chapter of this book, we describe our overall perspective. We specify what negotiating rationally is and why you need this skill. The rest of the book is organized in three sections:

In the first, we answer the question: if you and your opponent don't negotiate rationally, what errors can you expect? What can you do to eliminate them? We provide examples that let you audit your own decision processes in two-party negotiation.

In the second, we outline general frameworks for thinking more rationally about negotiation. We focus on one particular negotiation to guide you through the necessary steps you must take to evaluate when and how to reach an agreement, and when to walk away—in both cases, producing outcomes that are in your best interest.

In the third, we go beyond the standard two-party negotiation and look at the variety of settings and contexts in which executives must rationally negotiate with multiple opponents, issues, and constraints. Some factors we consider are expertise, emotion and fairness, multiple parties, negotiating through third parties, competitive bidding, and negotiating through action.

Finally, we close with advice on how to negotiate with irrational opponents and how to make all that you've learned about rational negotiation an integral part of your behavior.

Acknowledgments

We started developing our framework for thinking rationally in negotiation over a decade ago. Throughout this process, we were guided by the research and writings of Howard Raiffa, Danny Kahneman, and Amos Tversky. There is no way that we can present the research on which these ideas are based to adequately recognize the contributions of our coauthors, whose ideas are now so intertwined with our own, we often fail to fully recognize their unique contribution. Our associations with Jeanne Brett, Jack Brittain, John Carroll, Tina Diekmann, Vandra Huber, George Loewenstein, Beta Mannix, Keith Murnighan, Greg Northcraft, Robin Pinkley, Jeff Polzer, Harris Sondak, Leigh Thompson, Tom Tripp, Kathleen Valley, and Sally White have influenced every idea in this book and have informed and shaped our research and broadened our perspective. Finally, we owe an intellectual debt to a number of negotiation scholars who have helped to create the field of negotiations. These include the timeless classic of Richard Walton and Robert McKersie, as well as the more recent writings of Tom Kochan, Harry Katz, Roy Lewicki, Dean Pruitt, Larry Susskind, and Jeff Rubin.

Every sentence, every paragraph, and every chapter in this book has been rewritten more times than we care to remember. Authors are notorious for being nervous about what editors will do to their ideas. Our experience with editors has been wonderful. Every time Claire Buisseret, Bob Wallace, Nancy Vergara, Val Poirier, and especially Pam Jiranek and John Lavine touched the manuscript, we were delighted to see how much better our ideas could be expressed. Editing is an important talent, and we have been fortunate to be surrounded by wonderful editors. In addition, our pharmaceutical case in Part II also benefited from the expertise of Gene Watkins, Jon Tanja, and Ed Zajac.

A number of excellent institutions have also helped this project along. The J.L. Kellogg Graduate School of Management at Northwestern University continues to be a wonderful place to do work on the topic of negotiation. The interest in negotiation created by Jeanne Brett, the support of Dean Donald Jacobs, the spectacular group of doctoral students, and the creation of the Dispute Resolution Research Center (funded by the Hewlett Foundation) have made Kellogg a truly unique academic environment. In addition, our teaching experience with over ten thousand MBA and executive students at Kellogg has dramatically improved the clarity of our advice. We also had the opportunity to develop cases and ideas under the support of the Newspaper Management Center at Northwestern University (directed by John Lavine).

We were supported by the J. Jay Gerber and J.L. Kellogg Distinguished Professorships. Our research has also benefited from the support of research grants provided by the National Science Foundation, National Institute for Dispute Resolution, the Fund for Research in Dispute Resolution, Northwestern University Research Grants Committee, and Eller Center for the Study of the Private Market Economy (Arizona). This book was begun while Max was a fellow at the Center for Advanced Study in the Behavioral Sciences, a wonderful place to start a writing project. His funding there was partially provided by the Russell Sage Foundation and the National Science Foundation.

We close our acknowledgments by reemphasizing the debt that we owe our colleagues for the critical role that they have played in the development of this book and our perspective on negotiation. Our research group on cognition and rationality in negotiation is simply amazing. We could hope for no better group of collaborators, and we close by dedicating this book to Beta Mannix, Greg Northcraft, Leigh Thompson, Kathleen Valley, and Sally White.

CHAPTER

1

Introduction to Rational Thinking in Negotiation

Everyone negotiates.
While many people think of negotiation as something that takes place only between a buyer and a seller or a union and management, in its various forms, negotiation is used every day to resolve differences and allocate resources. It occurs between all sorts of people—colleagues, spouses, children, neighbors, strangers, corporate entities, even nations negotiate. Some negotiations are face-to-face; others take place over time through sequential decisions between competitors. In business, millions of negotiations happen every day, often within the same company.

Think of all the times you negotiate. What could be more central to business than negotiation? And what could be more central to successful negotiation than casting off your illusions about it and, henceforth, negotiating *rationally* and effectively? This book will teach you how to do just that.

Negotiating rationally means making the best decisions to *maximize* your interests. However, we are not concerned with "getting to yes."[1] Our work shows that in many cases, no agreement at all is better than "getting to yes." What we've learned from thousands of executives will help you decide when it's smart to reach an agreement and when it is *not*.

Negotiating rationally means knowing how to reach the *best* agreement, not just any agreement. What we've learned will help you avoid decisions that leave both you and those you negotiate with worse off.

1

All executives have pervasive decision-making biases that blind them to opportunities and prevent them from getting as much as they can out of a negotiation. They include the following:

1. Irrationally escalating your commitment to an initial course of action, even when it is no longer the most beneficial choice
2. Assuming your gain must come at the expense of the other party, and missing opportunities for trade-offs that benefit both sides
3. Anchoring your judgments upon irrelevant information, such as an initial offer
4. Being overly affected by the way information is presented to you
5. Relying too much on readily available information, while ignoring more relevant data
6. Failing to consider what you can learn by focusing on the other side's perspective
7. Being overconfident about attaining outcomes that favor you

Keep these seven factors in mind as you consider the following example.

In 1981 American Airlines introduced its frequent-flier program, arguably the most innovative marketing program in the history of the airline industry. Business fliers (or anyone else who flew frequently) could earn miles for the flights they took and redeem those miles for travel awards. While the incentive plan— designed to encourage loyalty for American—may have seemed like a brilliant marketing strategy, it was a miserable decision from a negotiations standpoint and soon proved disastrous from a marketing and financial standpoint.

Following American's lead, every airline in the industry soon launched its own frequent-flier program. Increasing the competition further, each company soon offered double miles to their most frequent passengers and even more miles for hotel stays, car rentals, etc. Soon, the benefits required to remain competitive inflated out of control and resulted in tremendous liabilities. By December 1987, when Delta announced that all passengers who charged tickets to their American Express card would get *triple* miles for all of 1988, analysts estimated that the airlines owed their passengers between $1.5 and $3 *billion* in free trips. How could the airlines get out of this mess?

One possible answer comes from a similar competitive war that took place in the United States auto industry in 1986. All three U.S. auto companies were engaged in rebate programs designed to increase their sales volume and market share. The rebate each company offered swiftly escalated. As soon as one manufacturer raised its offer, the rest followed, and the profits of all three companies plummeted. Each then added the option of discount financing for their customers as an alternative to a rebate. Again, the competition was fierce. It reached a point where U.S. auto makers were, on the average, losing money on every car sold. It takes no business sense to know that selling more can't make up for selling at a loss!

How could any one company escape this deadly spiral without losing market share to the other two?

Lee Iacocca, the CEO and chair of Chrysler, came up with a solution. He told the press that all three companies' programs were scheduled to expire in the near future and Chrysler had no plans to continue; however, if either of the other two continued their programs, Iacocca would meet or beat any promotion offered. What was his message to Ford and GM? Chrysler was proposing a cease-fire if the others cooperated, but threatening to retaliate if they continued to fight. Ford and GM got the message, and the rebate/financing program stopped.

What if United or American Airlines had made an announcement like Iacocca's before Delta announced triple miles? Delta would most likely have realized there was nothing to gain by the triple-mile promotion. Yet, the airlines failed to negotiate rationally because, unlike Iacocca, they did not consider the possible decisions of their competitors. Iacocca developed a negotiation strategy that explicitly attempted to manage his competitor's decisions. In contrast, the airlines ignored the decisions of their competitors, and airline debt went up significantly, with some estimates placing it as high as $12 billion.[2] Mark Lacek, director of business-travel marketing at Northwest Airlines lamented the triple-mileage promotions in 1988: "It's suicide marketing. Insanity."[3] According to *Fortune,* "In the annals of marketing devices run amok, few can compare to the airlines' wildly popular frequent flier plans."[4]

You will find that this book analyzes why many executives make mistakes like the airlines did, how some—like the auto companies—avoid disastrous pitfalls, and, most important, how you can solve your own negotiating problems. From big negotiations between companies to tough personal ones between you and a colleague or someone you love, we'll help you learn to solve them rationally—and more effectively. We will guide you through a variety of thought processes to minimize the type of "competitive irrationality" just described in the airline example.

Now let's be honest. There are lots of books on negotiation. Some are smart; some are not. Our book, however, is not based solely on our academic experience—it's based on our working with and observing closely thousands of executives and bringing together information from similar studies done with working executives who must make countless decisions involving negotiations every day.

This book is not ivory-tower theory. It is information from the trenches for use by real managers who want to be more effective. (If you are interested in learning more about the theory behind the studies, however, the endnotes will refer you to the right sources.)

Many bright and successful people make mistakes in negotiation. And no book can make you a flawless negotiator. However, a clearer understanding of rational negotiation will make you a far more effective one. To that end, we introduce two strategies to increase your effectiveness. The first helps you see the common mistakes made in negotiation. The second identifies ways to eliminate those mistakes and offers a straightforward framework to help you become a more rational negotiator.

The aspect of negotiation that an executive can control most directly is *how* s/he makes decisions. The parties, the issues, and the negotiation environment are often beyond your control. Rather than seeking to change them, you must improve your ability to make effective, more rational decisions—to negotiate *smarter*.

There are psychological limits to a negotiator's effectiveness. A psychological perspective is also required to best anticipate the likely decisions and subsequent behavior of the other party. In the following chapters, we will show you how various factors—such as how you structure problems, process information, frame the situation, and evaluate alternatives—can influence your judgment as a negotiator and limit your effectiveness.

Negotiation is challenging and exciting. It should also be one of the most honed and effective tools in your arsenal. The ideas presented in this book will go a long way toward putting you on a level with the best negotiators we've seen.

ONE

Common Mistakes in Negotiation

CHAPTER

2

The Irrational Escalation of Commitment

People often behave in ways inconsistent with their own self-interests. One common mistake is to irrationally stay committed to an initial course of action. Consider the following case.

The Campeau-Federated Merger

In 1987 Robert Campeau, then one of *Fortune*'s "Fifty Most Interesting Business People," sought to acquire the nation's most profitable department store, Bloomingdale's, both for its value and its drawing power for the shopping malls he planned to build. On 25 January 1988 he initiated a hostile takeover bid for Bloomingdale's parent company, Federated Department Stores.

A highly public bidding war developed between Campeau and Macy's over what was to become the largest and most visible retail merger in history. By March 25, the *Wall Street Journal* observed that "we're not dealing in price anymore but egos. What's been offered is top dollar, and beyond what anyone expected."[1] As this was going on, however, Federated's value was decreasing as managers defected and as plans concerning upcoming purchases and promotional expenditures collapsed.[2]

On March 31, with Macy's on the verge of winning the bidding war, Campeau approached them with an eleventh-hour offer to cede victory if Macy's would sell him Bloomingdale's and Burdines.[3] Macy's refused!

9

Campeau retaliated by topping Macy's already high offer by roughly $500 million. With this irrational act, Campeau won the battle, but lost the war. In January 1990, he declared bankruptcy.

This is the story of many merger battles. The desire to "win" at any cost preempts developing a rational negotiation strategy. This recklessness is one reason why acquirers tend to lose money in the merger-and-acquisition process. While many argue that mergers create synergy, the beneficiaries of this synergy are usually the targets, not the acquirers.[4]

Maxwell House and *Folgers* have battled for over ten years to dominate the U.S. coffee market. In addition to using costly incentives, both companies spent $100 million on coffee advertising in 1990 alone, roughly four times what they spent only three years earlier. This escalation has depressed prices to a level that hurts the entire industry, and neither Maxwell House nor Folgers has significantly improved its market share.

Competition of this type is common. The story of the coffee wars is also the story of the cola wars (Pepsi/Coke) and the camera wars (Polaroid/Kodak). Each side views its goal as beating the other firm as opposed to making the industry more profitable. While the information often exists to pursue a rational end to the conflict, each side sticks with its initial course of action, and catastrophe follows. Campeau went bankrupt. American coffee makers continue to lose millions of dollars in opportunity costs. Even when conflict is not leading to the desired outcome, decision makers are often obsessed by the small probability that escalating the conflict one step further could lead to victory.

We define *irrational escalation* as continuing a previously selected course of action beyond what rational analysis would recommend. Misdirected persistence can lead to wasting a great deal of time, energy, and money.[5] Directed persistence can lead to commensurate payoffs. Rational analysis enables you to distinguish the two.

You must recognize that the time and money already invested are "sunk costs." They *cannot* be recovered and should *not* be considered when selecting future courses of action. Your reference point for action should be the present. Consider your alternatives by evaluating only the *future* costs and benefits associated with each.

This is a hard concept to absorb. Once committed to a course of action, executives often allocate resources in ways that justify their previous choices, whether or not they now appear valid.[6] This tendency exists in financial and military situations, as well as in common day-to-day managerial experiences.[7] For example, the manager who hires an employee behaves differently from those who did not, regardless of the employee's level of performance. S/he will negotiate harder for that employee, evaluate that employee more favorably, provide larger rewards to that employee, and make more optimistic projections of that employee's future performance—all to justify the initial hiring decision.

THE $20 BILL AUCTION

Imagine you are in a room with thirty people. Someone at the front of the room takes a twenty dollar bill from his or her pocket and announces the following:

> I am about to auction off this twenty dollar bill. You are free to participate in the bidding or just watch. People will be invited to call out bids in multiples of one dollar until no further bidding occurs, at which point the highest bidder will pay the amount bid and win the twenty dollars. The only feature that distinguishes this auction from traditional auctions is a rule that the second highest bidder must also pay the amount he or she bid, but he or she will obviously not win the twenty. For example, if Bill bid $3 and Jane bid $4, and bidding stopped, I would pay Jane $16 ($20 less $4) and Bill, the second highest bidder, would pay me $3.

> Would you be willing to bid $1 to start the auction?

> (Make this decision before reading further.)

We've run this auction with investment bankers, consultants, physicians, professors, partners in Big Six accounting firms, lawyers, and assorted other executives. The pattern is always the same. The bidding starts out fast and furious until the bidding reaches the $12 to $16 range. At this point, everyone except the two highest bidders drops out. The two bidders left feel the trap. If one has bid $16 and the other $17, the $16 bidder must either bid $18 or suffer a $16 loss. Bidding further, a choice that *might* produce a gain if the other person quits, seems more attractive than certain loss, so he or she bids $18. When the bids are $19 and $20, surprisingly, the rationale to bid $21 is very similar to all previous decisions—you can accept a $19 loss or continue and hope to reduce your loss. Of course, the rest of the group roars with laughter when the bidding goes over $20—which it nearly always does. Obviously, the bidders are acting irrationally. But what are the irrational bids?

Skeptical readers should try out the auction on their friends, co-workers, or students. Final bids in the $30 to $70 range are common, and our most successful auction sold a $20 bill for $407 (the final bids were $204 and $203). We've earned over $10,000 running these auctions in classes over the last four years.

The dollar auction paradigm, first introduced by Martin Shubik,[8] helps explain why people escalate their commitment to a previously selected course of action.[9] Participants naïvely enter the auction not expecting the bidding to exceed the true value of the object ($20)—"After all, who would bid more than $20 for $20?" The potential gain, coupled with the possibility of "winning" the auction, is reason enough to enter. Once in the auction, it takes only a few extra dollars for the bidder to stay in rather than accept a sure loss. This "reasoning," along with a strong need to justify entering the auction in the first place, keeps most bidders bidding.

Clearly, once someone else bids it creates a problem. A bidder may feel that one more bid may get the other person to quit. If *both* bidders feel this way, the result can be catastrophic. Yet, without knowing what to expect from the other bidder, continued bidding is not clearly wrong. So what is the bidder's solution?

The key is to recognize the auction as a trap and never to make even a very small bid. Successful managers must learn to identify traps. One strategy is to try to consider the decision from the perspective of the other decision maker(s). In the dollar auction, this strategy would quickly tell you that the auction looks just as attractive to other bidders as it does to you. With this knowledge, you can predict what will happen and stay out.

Similar traps exist in business, war, and our personal lives. It could be argued that in the Gulf war, Iraq's leader Saddam

Hussein had the information necessary to pursue a negotiated settlement rationally. The initial "investment" incurred by invading Kuwait trapped him into further escalating his commitment not to compromise.

Two gasoline stations in a price war can also find themselves in the dollar auction trap. The price of gasoline is $1.30/gallon. Your competitior decides to drive you out of business; you would like to drive her out of business. She drops the price to $1.25/gallon. You drop the price to $1.20/gallon—your break-even point. She drops her price to $1.15/gallon. What's your next move? You may both suffer tremendously trying to win a price war, and, as in the dollar auction, neither of you is likely to win the competition on price alone.

WHY DOES ESCALATION OCCUR?

To eliminate irrational escalation you must understand the psychological factors that feed it. When you commit yourself to a course of action, this commitment biases your perception and judgment, causes you to make irrational decisions to manage the impressions of others, and leads to a competitive escalatory spiral.

BIASES IN PERCEPTION AND JUDGMENT

Once Robert Campeau decided to try to acquire Federated, he probably considered data that supported and confirmed that decision, and ignored data that contradicted it. Most people do this. It's easy to identify this "confirmation trap." You make a tentative decision (e.g., to buy a new car, to hire a particular employee, to start research and development on a new product line). Do you search for data that supports your decision before making the final commitment? Most do. Do you search for data that challenges it? Most do not. A manager committed to a basic strategy is likely to be biased in favor of the data consistent with it.

You must recognize this bias and search vigilantly for disconfirming information, as well as the confirming data you intuitively seek. Establishing monitoring systems to check your perceptions before you make a judgment or decision can be useful. An objective outsider, for example, can help you reduce or eliminate any bias against disconfirming information.

Besides limiting your perception, your initial commitment also biases any subsequent judgments you make. That is, an executive in a negotiation tends to form expectations that justify decisions consistent with his or her initial course of action. Any loss from an initial investment (such as bidding $21 for a twenty dollar bill) distorts judgment in favor of continuing to bid. Campeau's biased judgment about the future of the merged company justified his actions in his own mind.

IMPRESSION MANAGEMENT

Even if Campeau knew that Federated was no longer worth what it would cost him to acquire it, he had to defend his reputation with his critical stakeholders. Perhaps losing to Macy's was unacceptable in light of the impression Campeau wanted to convey. People not only selectively perceive information, but they also selectively provide information to others. Thus they are more likely to provide confirming, rather than disconfirming information about initial decisions. Maybe Campeau was motivated to provide his stakeholders with information that confirmed the rationality of his acquisition strategy.

People don't want to admit failure. They like to appear consistent, and the consistent course of action is to increase commitment to previous actions. Consistency in both organizational and personal interactions is strongly reinforced in society. Barry Staw and Jerry Ross argue that people prefer leaders who are consistent in their actions to leaders who switch from one line of behavior to another.[10] Inconsistency was cited as the second most common reason for dissatisfaction with President Carter in the Gallup Poll collected after his first year in office.[11] Similarly, John F. Kennedy states in *Profiles in Courage* that one of the most courageous decisions politicians ever have to make is to choose an action they believe is in the best interests of their constituency, yet one they know that very same constituency won't like. As suggested above, that conflict is particularly severe if that choice is also seen as inconsistent.

The result is an interesting paradox: The best choice for your organization means making the best decision based on future costs and benefits, and ignoring any previous commitments. Yet, you may be rewarded more for sticking with earlier, bad decisions that convey an impression of consistency. Organizations need to create systems that reward good decision making over effective impression management. First, those in charge must convey to everyone that impression management at the expense of high-quality decisions won't be tolerated. Second, an organization must establish reward systems that bring the employees' values closer to the organization's. In short, if the organization wants its managers to make good decisions, then good decision making must be what is best for its managers' future careers.

Evaluating decisions on process rather than outcome is consistent with Peters and Waterman's discussion, in *In Search of Excellence,* of Heinz's experimentation with "perfect failures."[12] The perfect failure concept recognizes that many decisions are inherently risky. In fact, Peters and Waterman say that management should learn to recognize how much can be learned through failures and celebrate when they occur! The central point is that managers must learn to recognize good choices, not just good outcomes.

COMPETITIVE IRRATIONALITY

Competitive irrationality occurs when two parties act in a clearly irrational manner in terms of the expected outcomes, but it's hard to identify any specific actions as irrational. Many would argue that even entering the $20 auction is irrational. This may be reasonable, but it's not completely valid. If it makes no sense for you to play, then it makes no sense for anyone to play. But if no one else plays, you can bid a small amount and get a bargain. While this sounds logical, once you make the initial bid, someone else bids, and the bind we've already described appears.

We argued earlier that continuing to bid will then depend on whether you think the other bidder is likely to quit. Obviously, the same reasoning applies to the other person. If someone can get $20, for $1, it must be rational for one person to bid. Yet, you know what happens when several people think this way. Thus, in many ways, competitive irrationality is an unresolved paradox, rather than an explanation of escalation. You should remember that many situations look like opportunities, but prove to be traps if you don't fully consider the possible actions of others.

CHAPTER

3

The Mythical Fixed-Pie

The best negotiations end in a resolution that satisfies all parties. Such agreements are rare. More commonly, successful negotiations end in trade-offs. Where each party gives up something of lesser value to them in return for something of greater. Because people often value the multiple issues in a negotiation differently, trade-offs can speed up and improve a conflict's resolution.

A *distributive* negotiation usually involves a single issue—a "fixed-pie"—in which one person gains at the expense of the other. For example, haggling over the price of a rug in a bazaar is a distributive negotiation. In most conflicts, however, more than one issue is at stake, and each party values the issues differently. The outcomes available are no longer a fixed-pie divided among all parties. An agreement can be found that is better for both parties than what they would have reached through distributive negotiation. This is an *integrative* negotiation.

However, parties in a negotiation often don't find these beneficial trade-offs because each *assumes* its interests *directly* conflict with those of the other party. "What is good for the other side must be bad for us" is a common and unfortunate perspective that most people have. This is the mind-set we call the *mythical* "fixed-pie."

For example, it's Friday evening and you and your spouse are going to dinner and a movie. Unfortunately, you prefer different restaurants and different movies. It's easy to think of the negotiation as purely distributive—your choices are at your spouse's expense—and compromise on both issues. But if you look beyond the fixed-pie and consider how much you value each of your choices, you may discover that you care more about choosing the restaurant and your spouse cares more about choosing the movie. That way, you can find a restaurant and movie combination that you each value over a compromise. This is an integrative agreement.

Business negotiations also provide opportunities for mutually beneficial trade-offs. Consider the following problem:

> A large corporation (CORP) wanted to make a friendly acquisition of one of its suppliers, a privately held company (PRIVATE). Both agreed that PRIVATE would be more valuable as a part of CORP. Despite this agreement, they were unable to complete the acquisition. CORP had offered $14 million for PRIVATE, but PRIVATE had insisted on $16 million. Efforts at a compromise price failed. Neither side found a $15 million price acceptable.

With both sides expecting PRIVATE to be worth more as part of CORP, how could both find the $15 million price unacceptable? The two parties had very different views of the value of a new high-tech, high-risk entrepreneurial division (Venture) of PRIVATE. CORP considered Venture worth only $1 million (of the $14 million offered), while PRIVATE truly believed in the viability of the new products under development and had valued this division at $6 million. When they realized they could trade-off on this underlying issue, they had found their solution. CORP acquired PRIVATE for $12 million, but the owners of PRIVATE retained control of Venture. From CORP's perspective, this agreement was even better than acquiring the entire company for $14 million. From PRIVATE's perspective, this agreement was better than the $16 million that they demanded since they still owned Venture, which they valued at $6 million.

Negotiations are more than simply a fight over who gets how much of the pie. While parties often have several interests in a negotiation, they rarely evaluate the relative importance of each. If you clearly identify your priorities before a negotiation, you can find effective trade-offs by conceding less important issues to gain on more important ones.

The fixed-pie assumption leads managers to interpret most competitive situations as win-lose, an orientation that's reinforced in our society by such traditions as athletic competition, admission to academic programs, and corporate promotion systems. People often generalize from these objective win-lose situations to others that are not necessarily win-lose. When both cooperation and competition are required, the competitive outlook dominates, resulting in a fixation on the distributive approach to bargaining. This inhibits the creative problem-solving necessary to develop integrative solutions.

People often fail to solve problems because of the assumptions they place on them.[1] Attempt to draw four (and only four) straight lines that connect all nine dots shown here without lifting your pencil (or pen) from the paper.[2]

• • •

• • •

• • •

People typically try the following solutions.

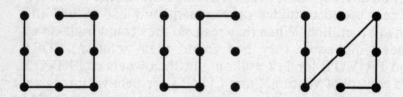

Most people try to use their logical decision skills on the *perceived* problem: connecting all nine dots without going outside the boundaries they imply. People make an *assumption* that frames the problem, but keeps them from finding a solution. *This is the most critical barrier to creative problem solving.* People tend to make false assumptions about problems to fit them into their previously established expectations. However, successful *creative* solutions often lie outside these self-imposed assumptions.

For example, once you discard the assumption about the barrier around the nine dots, you should find it fairly easy to come up with a solution similar to this one:

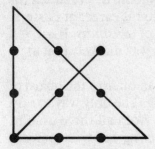

Negotiation is, in some ways, a kind of creative problem solving. To "connect the dots" managers must not assume a mythical fixed-pie, rather, they should look for trade-offs. Finding trade-offs is quite easy if you think to look for them, and quite difficult if you make inappropriate assumptions about the other side's interests.

The pervasiveness and destructiveness of the mythical fixed-pie is captured in the words of South Carolina Congressman Floyd Spence, who said in discussing a proposed SALT treaty: "I have had a philosophy for some time in regard to SALT, and it goes like this: the Russians will not accept a SALT treaty that is not in their best interest, and it seems to me that if it is in their best interest, it can't be in our best interest."[3] The assumption that anything good for the Soviet Union must be bad for the United States is a very clear expression of the mythical fixed-pie. Most political experts, on both sides of the political fence, would agree that the cooperation that has developed between the United States and the Soviet Union over the past few years has been to the benefit of both.

The mythical fixed-pie is a fixation equally prevalent in the business world. In late 1985, the president of Eastern Airlines, Frank Borman (the former astronaut), aware of the company's poor financial condition, presented the airline's three major unions with an ultimatum—if they did not agree to significant wage concessions, he would sell the airline.[4] The unions didn't take him seriously. They had valid contracts for an extended period and did not believe Borman wanted to give up control of the airline. But they became anxious when Borman began discussions with Frank Lorenzo, the most feared executive in the industry. Lorenzo had busted the unions at Continental, and had a general reputation as the most ruthless dictator in the corporate world. The only problem was that Borman had no desire to sell the airline to Lorenzo; it would be a bitter end to his career at Eastern. "What's more," argued Aaron Bernstein of *Business Week*, "if Borman gave up his command of Eastern, it was unlikely that at 57 he'd have anywhere else to go."[5]

Once discussions started, Lorenzo made an offer to the board of directors that forced them to consider selling. The only way to save Eastern was to obtain significant wage cuts from all three unions. While the pilots' and flight attendants' unions agreed to 20 percent wage cuts, the machinists' union, headed by militant Charlie Bryan, would only accept a 15 percent cut. Borman demanded 20 percent. Neither would move. Both argued that the failure of the other side to make a further concession would destroy the airline. They played a game of chicken, and no one chickened out.[6] When the deadline on the Lorenzo offer arrived without any agreement between Borman and the machinists, the board accepted Lorenzo's offer.

The irrationality in this outcome for both Borman and the machinists is evident. Lorenzo forced wage cuts, eliminated jobs, and eventually destroyed the airline.

Why was the airline ever sold to Lorenzo? Largely because Borman and Bryan both assumed mythical fixed-pies in the negotiation. Both negotiated as if the only way to gain was for the other side to lose. They never seriously considered negotiation strategies that would work to the advantage of both sides. They were under incredible pressure, but that simply increases the importance of finding a solution that works to the advantage of both parties. Limited by their assumptions, they ended up with an impasse and never discovered the many integrative trade-offs that would have benefited them both.

People who assume mythical fixed-pies will not find mutually beneficial trade-offs. However, consider what can happen even when both parties have identical preferences on a specific issue. For example, a company wants its workers to be better trained to increase work flexibility, while the workers want to be better trained to increase their employment security. Psychologist Leigh Thompson has found that even when the two sides want the same thing, they often settle for a different outcome because they assume that they must compromise to get agreement.[7] "If I want more training, they must not want me to get more training." This leads to what Thompson calls the "incompatibility bias"—the assumption that one side's interests are incompatible with the other's.

In a negotiation simulation involving eight issues, Thompson included two issues that were compatible—the parties had the same preference. Rationally, there was nothing to negotiate. Yet, 39 percent of the negotiations failed to result in the mutually preferred outcome on at least one of the two compatible issues. Further, even when the two sides reached an optimal agreement, neither realized that the other party had also benefited. Such a misperception in a negotiation can give an executive inflated confidence in his or her persuasive and bargaining abilities.[8]

The mythical fixed-pie also causes managers to "reactively devalue" any concession simply because it's offered by an adversary.[9] Connie Stillinger and her colleagues divided 137 individuals into two groups and asked how favorable an arms reduction proposal would be to the United States and to the U.S.S.R. One group was told (correctly) the proposal came from Mr. Gorbachev. The other group was told that President Reagan (the study was conducted during his presidency) had made the proposal. Fifty-six percent of those who believed the proposal was Gorbachev's thought it dramatically favored the Russians. Only 16 percent felt that it favored the U.S. The other 28 percent thought that it favored both sides equally. In the group that believed Reagan had initiated the proposal, 45 percent thought it benefited both sides equally, 27 percent thought that it favored the U.S.S.R, and 27 percent thought it favored the United States. Thus, terms that appear beneficial when advanced by one's own side may seem disadvantageous when proposed by the other party, even if the terms are equal. This is consistent with the inherent flaw in the mythical fixed-pie perception—what is good for them must be bad for us.

Managers commonly ask "What should we discuss first in a negotiation?" Some managers believe it is critical to get the most important issue resolved in the beginning as "any other strategy is simply procrastinating." In labor relations, many experienced negotiators recommend "starting with the easy issues first," an institutionalized step in the folklore of labor-management negotiations. Unfortunately, neither view is good advice. Both strategies eliminate possible trade-offs that may create joint benefits. Once resolved, an issue is rarely resurrected to be used in a trade-off.

Advice to solve the easy issues or hard issues first is still taken seriously because of the persistence of the mythical fixed-pie mind-set. But when each side values the issues differently, it is essential to deal with alternative "packages" that allow for the simultaneous discussion of multiple issues. How to build integrative-agreement packages will be discussed later. For now, we simply want you to note the prevalence of the mythical fixed-pie in negotiation decisions.

CHAPTER

4

Anchoring and Adjustment

Many factors influence the initial positions people take when entering a negotiation. To proceed, both sides must adjust their positions throughout the negotiation, ultimately arriving at either agreement or impasse. The initial positions act as anchors and affect each side's perception of what outcomes are possible.

In the previous chapter, we described how a fixed-pie bias resulted in the takeover of Eastern Airlines by Frank Lorenzo. Lorenzo's own anchoring and adjustment bias led to his eventual removal from Eastern.

When Lorenzo took over Eastern in 1985, he believed the fastest way to turn the company around was to reduce labor costs. However, the machinists', pilots', and flight attendants' unions refused to submit their contracts to renegotiation. Meanwhile, Lorenzo's goal seemed to change from reducing labor costs for the economic health of Eastern to a crusade to rid Eastern of unions, regardless of the cost. While Lorenzo attempted to break the machinists' union, Eastern lost approximately $1 million a day. His approach reduced Eastern from being the third largest carrier to the seventh, and in March 1989, Eastern filed for bankruptcy.

Finally willing to consider selling Eastern, Lorenzo decided that Peter Ueberroth (former commissioner of baseball) was the only acceptable buyer. Selling to the unions or to a competitor such as Carl Icahn (TWA CEO and corporate raider) was not acceptable psychologically. Ueberroth put together a deal with Drexel Burnham. Lorenzo would agree to sell Eastern for $464 million: $200 million in cash, $79 million in Eastern assets of airport slots and gates, and $185 million in forgiveness of Texas Air's debt to Eastern.[1] But after a handshake agreement, Lorenzo raised the price, telling Ueberroth he could only have Eastern if he added an additional $40 million. Ueberroth withdrew his offer.

Persuaded to come back to the table, Ueberroth was able to secure the unions' cooperation. But after a revised offer was presented to the board, Lorenzo raised nine additional issues. At this point, the deal finally fell through.

The value of Eastern continued to fall. Nevertheless, the judge handling the bankruptcy was determined to sell the airline. Two months later, an interested buyer, Joseph J. Ritchie, and the unions proposed another deal to Lorenzo that, while clearly not equivalent to the Ueberroth offer, was still worth discussing. Ritchie expected to begin negotiation there; however, Lorenzo told him that Eastern was worth more now than when Ueberroth bid and it would take an equivalent bid just to open discussions. It was obvious Lorenzo would not consider selling at Ritchie's price, and it was equally obvious that it "was absurd to say that an airline that had barely flown for months was worth more than when it had been grounded for a few weeks."[2] After Lorenzo failed to reach agreement with Ritchie or to develop a plan to get Eastern flying again, the bankruptcy judge stripped him of his control over Eastern Airlines and replaced him with a court-appointed trustee.

The impact of prior offers is a powerful one. Lorenzo's reliance on Ueberroth's offer as an anchor was critical in his eventual removal from Eastern. Based on that anchor he adjusted Eastern's value insufficiently, and, while he was finally able to break the unions, he did so at Eastern's expense.

People estimate the values of unknown or uncertain objects or events by starting from an initial anchor value and adjusting from there. These anchors are typically based upon whatever information, relevant, or irrelevant, is handy or strategic. Frequently, an anchor will inhibit individuals from negotiating rationally.

In a study to evaluate the decisions made by auditors at Big Eight (now the Big Six) accounting firms, half of the auditors were given the following problem:[3]

It is well known that many cases of management fraud go undetected even when competent annual audits are performed. The reason, of course, is that Generally Accepted Auditing Standards are not designed specifically to detect executive-level management fraud. We are interested in obtaining an estimate from practicing auditors of the prevalence of executive-level management fraud as a first step in ascertaining the scope of the problem.

1. Based on your audit experience, is the incidence of significant executive-level management fraud more than 10 in each 1,000 firms (i.e., 1%) audited by Big Eight accounting firms? (Circle one number.)

   Yes, more than 10 in each 1,000 Big Eight clients have significant executive-level management fraud. 1

   No, fewer than 10 in each 1,000 Big Eight clients have significant executive-level management fraud. 2

2. What is your estimate of the number of Big Eight clients per 1,000 that have significant executive-level management fraud?

   (Fill in the blank below with the appropriate number.)
   _____ in each 1,000 Big Eight clients have significant executive-level management fraud.

Auditors in the second group were given the same problem except they were asked whether the fraud incidence was more or less than *200* in 1,000, rather than 10. Auditors in the first group estimated an average fraud incidence of 16.52 per 1,000, auditors in the second group estimated 43.11 per 1,000. These professional auditors had fallen victim to the irrational effects of anchoring and adjustment.

In the problem posed to the auditors, the number used as their anchor was not based on any meaningful statistics. If such randomly selected anchors can have an impact on judgments of value, consider the effect of a more relevant anchor. We decided to examine the impact of a common anchor in residential real estate negotiations: the listing price.[4]

LISTING OFFERS AS ANCHORS IN NEGOTIATION

With the cooperation of a real estate agent who had just put a house on the market, we asked a number of real estate brokers to evaluate the house. We also asked a separate group of brokers what information they used in valuing a piece of residential real estate and to give us an estimate of how accurately agents could appraise its value. This second group said that any deviation from the appraisal value of more than 5 percent would be highly unusual and easy to recognize.

To give each agent all the information they needed about the house, we created a ten-page packet of information that included (1) the standard Multiple Listing Service (MLS) listing sheet for the property, (2) a copy of the MLS summary of residential real estate sales for both the entire city and the immediate neighborhood of the house for the last six months, (3) information including listing price, square footage, and other characteristics of the property, and other property in the same neighborhood, divided into four categories: property currently for sale, property recently sold, property sold but the sale not complete, and property previously listed that did not sell, and (4) standard MLS listing information for other property in the immediate neighborhood currently for sale.

We divided up the packets into four groups and changed two pieces of information in each. After having the property independently valued by appraisers, we took their average value and set the listing price twelve percent higher than the appraised value, four percent higher, four percent lower, or twelve percent lower. We then changed the price per square foot so that it correctly reflected the listing price.

When the agents came to evaluate the house (in the normal course of their jobs), we gave them one of the four packets and asked them to estimate (1) the appraised value of the house, (2) an appropriate listing price for the house, (3) a reasonable price to pay for the house, and (4) the lowest offer they would accept if

they were the seller. We also asked them to identify from a list
the relevant considerations that had gone into their evaluation
and briefly describe the process they used to arrive at the four
figures.

When we analyzed the data from these real estate agents, we
came up with some very interesting results. Figure 4.1 illustrates
the responses of the real estate agents. The listing price had a
major impact on their valuation process; they were more likely to
have high estimates on all four prices when the listing price was
high than when it was low.

When we tried to figure out what information they thought they
were using, another interesting pattern emerged. Although it is
clear that listing price had played a big role in the agents'
evaluation's of the house, only 19 percent of the agents mentioned
listing price as a factor they considered and only 8 percent
indicated that listing price was one of their top three considerations. Interestingly, almost three-quarters of the agents reported
using a computational strategy to assess the value of the real

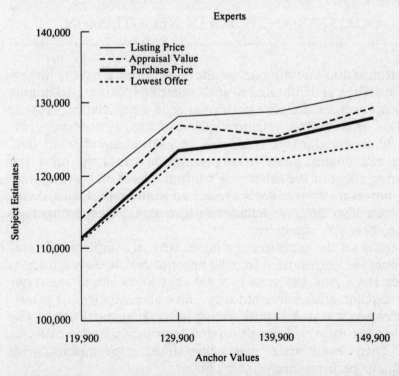

Figure 4.1 Listing Offers as Anchors in Real Estate Assessments

estate. To determine the value of the property, 72 percent of the agents indicated that they took the average price per square foot of comparable houses that had recently sold, multiplied that number by the number of square feet in our property and then adjusted for the condition of our house. If they had, indeed, used such a strategy, then we couldn't have observed any anchoring effect of the listing price; it would have been irrelevant. Nevertheless, the anchoring effect is not only present, it is pronounced.

Research has shown that final agreements in any negotiation are more strongly influenced by initial offers than by the subsequent concessionary behavior of an opponent,[5] particularly when issues under consideration are of uncertain or ambiguous value. Responding to an initial offer with suggested adjustments gives that anchor some measure of credibility. Thus, if an initial offer is too extreme, you need to re-anchor the process. Threatening to walk away from the table is better than agreeing to an unacceptable starting point.

GOALS AS ANCHORS IN NEGOTIATION

Both negotiation and managerial literature emphasize the importance of setting and adhering to goals.[6] Setting specific, challenging goals improves a manager's performance in a negotiation.[7] Just as initial offers can affect your perception of what is possible, goals affect what you think is attainable or even acceptable. In fact, setting challenging goals in a negotiation can help limit the anchoring effect of the other side's initial offer. Goal setting only helps, however, if your goals are set appropriately. Goals themselves can also become anchors, which can either hamper or enhance how you negotiate.

When we set the goals in our studies, we had complete information about the negotiation. In most negotiations, however, managers face large, obvious gaps in what they know about the other party, and sometimes in what they know about their own priorities or expectations. For goal setting to work to your benefit, the goals you set must sufficiently stretch your performance expectations. Then, even when you adjust those expectations, your subsequent performance remains high.

It's difficult for executives to know just how high to set goals, particularly in a negotiation. Because it's sometimes in your interest to hide certain information, it may be impossible to judge what is or is not a challenging goal prior to the negotiation. Thus, goal setting shares many of the problems associated with the anchoring and adjustment bias.

In a study we conducted, we assigned negotiators one of three levels of goals based on the difficulty of a task.[8] Easy goals were those that could be achieved by 99 percent of the negotiators; challenging goals, by approximately 75 percent of the negotiators; and difficult goals, by less than 5 percent of the negotiators. Once the negotiators had attempted the task, we asked them to assign their own, new goals for the same task. We found that those who were originally assigned easy goals set harder new goals, while negotiators originally assigned harder goals chose easier new goals. In spite of the adjustments, however, the new goals chosen by the easy-goal participants were significantly easier than the new, easier goals chosen by the difficult-goal participants. Thus, the initial goal levels not only anchored current performance but also the setting of goals for future performance.

CONCLUSIONS

In a negotiation, potential anchors are ubiquitous. They can be as relevant as previous contracts or as irrelevant as a random number. Even factors normally associated with improved performance, such as goals, can reduce an executive's effectiveness in a negotiation if not carefully crafted. Don't let an initial anchor minimize the amount of information and the depth of thinking you use to evaluate a situation, and don't give too much weight to an opponent's initial offer too early in the negotiation.

To use anchoring to your advantage, you must decide what initial offer will attract the attention of the other party. It can't be so extreme that the opponent won't even consider it. You want your offer to be attractive enough to your opponent to serve as an anchor for subsequent offers.

You are most susceptible to anchors during the initial stages of a negotiation; don't legitimize an unacceptable initial offer by making a counteroffer. Know enough about the disputed issues to recognize unrealistic anchors. If you prepare before a negotiation and are flexible during the negotiation, you can reduce the adverse impact of anchoring.

CHAPTER

5

Framing Negotiations

The way the options available in a negotiation are framed, or
presented, can strongly affect a manager's willingness to reach
an agreement. In this chapter, we identify some factors that
influence framing.

FRAMING THE SITUATION

Consider the following situation:[1]

> You are in a store, about to buy a new watch for $70. As you
> wait for the sales clerk, a friend of yours comes by and says
> she has seen an identical watch on sale for $40 in another
> store two blocks away. You know the service and reliability of
> the other store are just as good as this one. Will you travel
> two blocks to save $30?

Now consider this similar situation:

> You are in a store, about to buy a new video camera for $800.
> As you wait for the sales clerk, a friend of yours comes by
> and says she has seen an identical camera on sale for $770 in
> another store two blocks away. You know the service and
> reliability of the other store are just as good as this one. Will
> you travel two blocks to save the $30?

Nearly 90 percent of the managers presented with the first
problem said they would travel the two blocks. However, in the
second scenario, only about 50 percent of the managers would

31

make the trip. What makes the $30 so attractive in the first scenario and considerably less attractive in the second? One reason is that a $30 discount on a $70 watch is a very good deal; $30 off on an $800 video camera is not such a good deal. In evaluating your willingness to walk two blocks, you frame the options in terms of the percentage discount. Instead of considering whether the percentage discount is enough to make you go the other store, you should decide if the savings you get is greater than the value of the additional time you expect to invest. So, if a $30 savings was enough to justify walking two blocks for the watch, saving $30 on the video camera should also be worth the walk.

Here are two adapted versions of a problem Richard Thaler used to illustrate the influence of frames:[2]

> You are lying on the beach on a hot day. All you have to drink is ice water. For the last hour you've been thinking about how much you would enjoy a nice cold bottle of your favorite brand of beer. A companion gets up to make a phone call and offers to bring back a beer from the only place nearby where beer is sold: a fancy resort hotel. She says the beer might be expensive and asks how much you are willing to pay. She will buy the beer if it costs as much as or less than the price you say. But if it costs more, she won't buy it. You trust your friend and there is no possibility of bargaining with the bartender. What price are you willing to pay?

Now consider this version of the same story:

> You are lying on the beach on a hot day. All you have to drink is ice water. For the last hour you've been thinking about how much you would enjoy a nice cold bottle of your favorite brand of beer. A companion gets up to make a phone call and offers to bring back a beer from the only place nearby where beer is sold: a small, run-down grocery store. She says the beer might be expensive and asks how much you are willing to pay. She will buy the beer if it costs as much as or less than the price you say. But if it costs more, she won't buy it. You trust your friend and there is no possibility of bargaining with the store owner. What price are you willing to pay?

In both these stories, the results are the same: you get the same beer and there is no negotiating with the seller. Furthermore, the amenities of the resort are irrelevant since you will be drinking the beer on the beach. Our students were willing to pay significantly more if the beer were purchased at a "fancy resort hotel" ($7.83) than if the beer were purchased at the "small, run-down grocery store" ($4.10). This difference in price for the same beer is based upon the frame they put on the situation. Paying over $5 for a beer is an expected annoyance at a fancy resort hotel; paying over $5 for a beer at a run-down grocery store is an obvious "rip-off!" So, even though they got the same beer, without any of the benefits of the resort hotel, they were willing to pay almost three dollars more because of the way the purchase was framed.

The converse of this situation is probably familiar. Have you ever bought something because "it was too good a deal to pass up," even though you had no use for it? The frame of "a great deal" often has more value than what you actually buy.

FRAMING OUTCOMES

Amos Tversky and Daniel Kahneman presented a group of decision makers with the following problem:[3]

The U.S. is preparing for the outbreak of an unusual Asian disease that is expected to kill six hundred people. Two alternative programs are being considered. Which would you favor?

Half of the decision makers (Group I) were presented with two choices:

1. If Program A is adopted, two hundred people will be saved.
2. If Program B is adopted, there is a one-third probability that all will be saved and a two-thirds probability that none will be saved.

The other half (Group II) had these two choices:

1. If Program A is adopted, four hundred people will die.

2. If Program B is adopted, there is a one-third probability that no one will die and a two-thirds probability that all will die.

Of the 158 respondents in Group I, 76 percent chose Program A and 24 percent chose Program B. For Group I, the prospect of saving two hundred lives *for certain* was more valued than a risky prospect with equal expected value. Of the 169 respondents in Group II, 13 percent chose Program A and 87 percent chose Program B. This group preferred the risky, rather than the certain, alternative. The prospect of four hundred people dying *for certain* was less attractive than a lottery of equal expected value.

What caused Tversky and Kahneman's subjects to prefer the first outcome in Group I and the second outcome in Group II? To interpret these results, you need some understanding of how people respond to risk, and how your preference for risk can shift. People often identify themselves or others according to their attraction to risk. Paul Slovic, Baruch Fischhoff, and Sarah Lichtenstein argue that while a tendency to take or avoid risks may be one of the first factors people think of in describing someone's personality,[4] most people are not consistent in their approach to risk. When Slovic compared the scores of eighty-two people on nine different measures of risk taking, he found no evidence that risk taking was a stable personality characteristic,[5] which suggests that people who aggressively take risks in one situation may avoid risks in another. A professional gambler may be very careful about his or her health; a conservative financial analyst may let "all hell break loose" on weekends.

To define a manager's behavior in a negotiation as risk-averse, risk-neutral, or risk-seeking, you must look at the relationship between his or her *certainty equivalent* and the expected value of the available alternatives. For example, you have the opportunity to enter a lottery with a 50 percent chance of winning $10 million. What payoff would you demand to give up the option of playing the lottery? If you were risk-neutral, that payoff, your certainty equivalent, would be $5 million (the expected value of the lottery). Thus, a person with a certainty equivalent equal to the expected value of the lottery is *risk-neutral* with respect to playing. Someone with a certainty equivalent less than the expected value of the lottery is *risk-averse* to entering. If you were willing to accept $4 million instead of playing the lottery, you would be risk-averse because you are (theoretically) foregoing $1 million in expected value to avoid the lottery's risk. A certainty equivalent greater than the expected value of the lottery makes you *risk-seeking*. It takes more than the expected value of the lottery, perhaps $6,000,000, for you to give up both the excitement of gambling and your chance at winning.

In the Asian disease problem, it is obvious that identical questions were asked; however, by changing the description of the options from lives saved (a gain) to lives lost (a loss), the experimenters elicited very different risk preferences. This suggests that people are risk-averse when confronting potential gains and risk-seeking when confronting potential losses.[6]

The way information is framed in a negotiation can have a significant impact on a manager's preference for risk, particularly when s/he is uncertain about future events or outcomes. Managers can make irrational choices in a negotiation because their preference for risk can change, depending on the influence of a particular decision frame. The *referent point* you use to evaluate an alternative as either a gain or a loss determines the positive or negative frame imposed on your options and your subsequent willingness to accept or reject them.

FRAMING AND REFERENT POINTS

The choice of one referent point over another may be determined by a visible anchor, the "status quo," or by an invisible one, expectations. The status quo is one of the most common referent points. Most decision makers evaluate their options in terms of whether they represent a gain or a loss. Interestingly, it is surprisingly easy to modify what people include as part of their status quo.

THE ENDOWMENT EFFECT

In any exchange between a buyer and a seller, the buyer must be willing to pay at least the minimum amount the seller is willing to accept. An object's value to the seller may be determined by some objective third party such as an economic market. However, the seller often prices an item to include not only its market value but also a value for his or her emotional attachment to it. This added value is the *endowment effect.* The impact this effect has on the framing of the transaction was illustrated in a series of studies conducted by Daniel Kahneman, Jack Knetsch, and Richard Thaler.[7]

Imagine you've just been given a coffee mug.[8] (In the studies, coffee mugs were placed before one-third of the participants, the "sellers.") You are told that you "own the object (coffee mug) in your possession. You have the option of selling it if a price, to be determined later, is acceptable to you." Next, you are given a list (see table 5.1) of possible selling prices, ranging from $.50 to $9.50, and are told to indicate for each whether you would (a) sell the mug for that amount or (b) keep the mug and take it home with you. Take a minute to complete the form in table 5.1.

Another third of the group (the "buyers") were told they would be given a sum of money and they could either keep it or use it to buy a mug. They were also asked to indicate their preferences

---

Table 5.1 *Evaluating the Endowment Effect*

For each price listed below, indicate whether you would be willing to sell the coffee mug for that price or keep the mug.

If the price is $0.50, I will sell _____; I will keep the mug _____.
If the price is $1.00, I will sell _____; I will keep the mug _____.
If the price is $1.50, I will sell _____; I will keep the mug _____.
If the price is $2.00, I will sell _____; I will keep the mug _____.
If the price is $2.50, I will sell _____; I will keep the mug _____.
If the price is $3.00, I will sell _____; I will keep the mug _____.
If the price is $3.50, I will sell _____; I will keep the mug _____.
If the price is $4.00, I will sell _____; I will keep the mug _____.
If the price is $4.50, I will sell _____; I will keep the mug _____.
If the price is $5.00, I will sell _____; I will keep the mug _____.
If the price is $5.50, I will sell _____; I will keep the mug _____.
If the price is $6.00, I will sell _____; I will keep the mug _____.
If the price is $6.50, I will sell _____; I will keep the mug _____.
If the price is $7.00, I will sell _____; I will keep the mug _____.
If the price is $7.50, I will sell _____; I will keep the mug _____.
If the price is $8.00, I will sell _____; I will keep the mug _____.
If the price is $8.50, I will sell _____; I will keep the mug _____.
If the price is $9.00, I will sell _____; I will keep the mug _____.
If the price is $9.50, I will sell _____; I will keep the mug _____.

between a mug and sums of money ranging from $.50 to $9.50. The last third of the participants (the "choosers") were given a questionnaire indicating they would be given the option to receive either a mug or a sum of money. They also marked their preferences between the mug and sums between $.50 and $9.50. All participants were told their answers would not influence either the predetermined price of the mug or the amount of money to be received in lieu of the mug.

The sellers chose a median value of $7.12 for the mug, the buyers valued the mug at $2.88, and the choosers at $3.12. It is interesting that being a buyer or a chooser led to very similar evaluations of the mug's worth. However, for the sellers, owning the mug made it much more valuable—in this case, more than twice as valuable as either of other two groups considered it.

This disparity occurred because each role (buyer, seller, or chooser) created its own referent point. Owning something changes the nature of your relationship to it; giving it up is now seen as a loss. In valuing the item, you may include a dollar amount, an endowment, to offset that loss. The simple act of "owning" an item, however briefly, can increase your personal attachment to it and, once that attachment is formed, the perceived cost of breaking it is greater.

THE ARAB NEGOTIATION WITH SADDAM HUSSEIN

Consider an example of the endowment effect that has captured much of the world's attention in the early 1990s: Iraq's invasion of Kuwait.[9]

On 2 August 1990, Iraqi troops invaded Kuwait. Six days later, Iraqi president Saddam Hussein announced its outright annexation. In response, President Hosni Mubarak of Egypt called for an emergency Arab summit. By 30 August, the Arab League had held a series of meetings to develop a plan to defuse the situation.

The primary element of the plan was Iraq's agreement to withdraw its troops from Kuwait in exchange for a series of concessions. The first concession was maintaining possession of Bubiyan Island, an island in the Persian Gulf that blocks most of Iraq's short shoreline. Second, Iraq would be given the Ramaila oil fields, a site Iraq contends that Kuwait appropriated when it inched its oil wells onto the Iraqi side of the unmarked border. Third, Iraq's war debt to Kuwait from the Iran-Iraq war, which totaled some $14 billion, might be forgiven or renegotiated and/or Iraq would get "huge sums of money and possibly a permanent share of Kuwait's oil revenues."

The deal the Arab League offered Saddam Hussein was by far the best that he could have received, but he quickly dismissed the offer and kept his troops in Kuwait. Two factors in Saddam Hussein's evaluation process that may have led to his decision were the endowment effect and framing. Since he occupied Kuwait, all of its oil reserves and assets were his; any retreat from that position constituted certain loss. With the endowment effect working, the price offered by the Arab League was not enough to compensate Saddam Hussein for the loss of what was now part of his country.

But Saddam Hussein's options could have been framed differently. Suppose, instead of thinking in terms of giving up what was "his," he had looked at the Arab League offer as payment for two weeks' work. His perspective on the problem would have probably been very different. By removing the endowment effect and transforming the offer into a return-on-investment decision, his rejection of such a proposal, the best offer he'd get, would have been highly unlikely.

THE IMPACT OF FRAMING ON NEGOTIATION

To negotiate rationally, you must remember that the way in which a problem is framed or presented can dramatically alter how you perceive the value or acceptability of your alternatives. The risk-averse choice is to accept an offered settlement; the risk-seeking choice is to wait for potential future concessions. The particular referent point or base line you choose determines whether you will frame your decision as positive or negative.

Consider a labor-management contract negotiation. As the labor representative, you can view any offer from management in at least two ways, depending upon your referent point. If the referent point is the current contract, then you can evaluate management's offer in terms of the "gains" you can expect relative to the previous contract. If the referent point is your set of initial offers on the issues under consideration, then you are more likely to evaluate management's counteroffers in terms of the losses you will have to accept in order to reach agreement. Whether you view your options as losses or as gains will considerably influence your willingness to accept management's position—*even if the same options are offered in both cases.*

Likewise, the referent points available to someone negotiating the salary for a new position in a company include: (1) the current salary, (2) the company's initial offer, (3) the least he or she is willing to accept, (4) his or her estimate of the most the company is willing to pay, and (5) the initial salary request. As the job applicant's referent point moves from referent 1 to referent 5, he or she progresses from a positive to a negative frame in the negotiation. A modest *gain* compared to the current wage is perceived as a loss when compared to what he or she would like to receive. Employees currently making $15/hour and seeking an increase of $4/hour can view a proposed increase of $2/hour as a $2/hour gain in comparison to the current wage (referent 1) or as a $2/hour loss in comparision to their proposal of $19/hour (referent 5).

In a study of the impact of framing on collective bargaining outcomes, we staged a five-issue negotiation session with participants playing the roles of management or labor.[10] We manipulated each negotiator's frame by adjusting his or her referent point. We told half of the negotiators that any concessions they made from their initial offers represented losses to their constituencies (i.e., a negative frame). We told the other half that any agreements they were able to reach that were better than the current contract were gains to their constituencies (i.e., the positive frame). We found that negatively framed negotiators made fewer concessions and reached fewer agreements than positively framed negotiators. In addition, negotiators who had positive frames were more likely to perceive the negotiated outcomes as fair than those who had negative frames.

In another study, we posed the following problem to negotiators:

You are a wholesaler of refrigerators. Corporate policy does not allow any flexibility in pricing. There is flexibility in the expenses you can incur (shipping, financing terms, etc.), which have a direct effect on your profitability. You are negotiating an $8,000 sale. The buyer wants you to pay $2,000 in expenses; you want to pay less. When you negotiate the exchange, do you try to minimize your expenses by reducing them from $2,000, or maximize net profit (price less expenses) by increasing it from $6,000?

Again we found that the frame taken into the negotiation affected the behavior of the negotiators.[11] In this study, negotiators were led to view transactions in terms of either (1) net profit or (2) total expenses deducted from gross profits. Objectively, these two situations were identical. Maximizing profits and minimizing expenses achieve the same outcome. So, there is no reason to believe that a manager would behave differently if given the instructions to minimize expenses or to maximize profits.

Still, those negotiators told to maximize profit (i.e., a positive frame) were more concessionary. In addition, they completed significantly more transactions than their negatively framed counterparts (those told to minimize expenses). Because they completed more transactions, their overall profitability in the market was higher, even though the transactions completed by negatively framed negotiators showed a higher average profit.[12]

FRAMING, NEGOTIATOR BIAS, AND STRATEGIC BEHAVIOR

Framing can be strategically manipulated to direct performance in a negotiation. If you couch a proposal in terms of your opponents' potential gain, you can induce them to assume a positive frame of reference and thus make them more likely to make concessions. You can also emphasize the inherent risk in the negotiation situation for them and contrast that with the opportunity for a sure gain that you have offered.

Framing can also be important for mediators. If a mediator's strategy is to reach an agreement through compromise (we discuss mediation in detail in Chapter 15), he or she should help both parties see the negotiation from a positive frame. This is tricky, however, since the referent that creates a positive frame for one side is likely to lead to a negative frame for the other—if presented to both sides simultaneously. Framing may be most effective as a strategy when a mediator meets with each party separately. The mediator can present different perspectives to each party to create a positive frame, which then leads to the subsequent risk-averse behavior associated with such a frame. Additionally, the mediator should emphasize to both parties the possible losses to each side in continuing the dispute. These strategies can help both sides prefer the certainty of a settlement.

Being a buyer or seller creates a natural frame. Consider the curious and consistent finding in a number of studies that buyers tend to outperform sellers in market settings where the balance of power is equal.[13] Given the artificial context of laboratory markets, there is no logical reason why buyers should do better than sellers. One explanation, however, may be that sellers think about the transaction in terms of the dollars exchanged and conceptualize the process as gaining resources (e.g., how many dollars do I gain by selling the commodity). On the other hand, buyers may view the transaction in terms of the loss of dollars (e.g., how many dollars do I have to give up). If the dollars are the primary focus, then buyers would tend to be risk-seeking and sellers risk-averse.

When a risk-averse person negotiates with a risk-seeking person, the risk-seeker is more willing to risk the potential agreement by demanding more or being less concessionary. To reach agreement, the risk-averse person must make additional concessions to induce the other to accept the agreement. Thus, when relative achievements of buyers and seller can be directly compared, buyers would benefit from their negative frame (and subsequent risk-seeking behavior). The critical issue is that these naturally occurring frames can easily influence the way the disputed issues are perceived—even without the conscious intervention of one or more of the parties.

Frames in negotiations can make the difference between agreement and impasse. Both sides typically talk in terms of a certain wage, price, or outcome that they must get, setting a high referent point against which gains and losses are measured. Any compromise is perceived as a loss. This may lead executives in negotiations to adopt negative frames to all proposals, to exhibit risk-seeking behaviors, and to be less likely to reach settlement. Nevertheless, when negotiators maintain a risk-neutral or risk-seeking perspective in evaluating an opponent's proposals the agreements reached are often more profitable.

CHAPTER
6

Availability of Information

When managers evaluate information and options, they often pay attention to certain facts and ignore others. For example, an executive may rely too much on information that is easily available, regardless of its importance to the final outcome. This tendency often produces interesting behavior. Consider the earthquake scare that occurred in the Midwest during late 1990.

Iben Browning, a climatologist and business consultant from New Mexico, predicted that on 3 December 1990, because of "unusually high tidal forces," there was a 50 percent chance that an earthquake with a magnitude of 6.5 to 7.5 on the Richter scale would strike along the New Madrid fault line, which runs from Cairo, Illinois, to Marked Tree, Arkansas. While anyone can predict an earthquake and not make the news, the media paid particular attention to Browning because his prediction was made during the "Sweeps" week when the number of viewers for each television news show is measured. Many of the news programmers, especially those in the Midwest, thought this was just the story they needed to boost their ratings.

Although Browning's prediction was widely discounted by expert geologists as groundless,[1] the extensive publicity it received had a surprising impact. Illinois insurance companies did a booming business in earthquake

insurance. Allstate doubled the number of earthquake
policies written. State Farm Insurance received eleven
thousand earthquake insurance applications per week
during November 1990. The year before, only 10 percent
of State Farm's clients had earthquake insurance; by the
middle of November that figure had risen to 45 percent.

Some insurance agents were using the prediction to
actively promote earthquake insurance. Two companies,
Berent and Co. and Hallberg Insurance Company, sent out
warnings to their clients to check their policies to ensure
that they covered earthquakes. Both companies justified
these communications as part of their responsibility to
inform their clients of "proper coverage" and the
limitations of their current policies.

Of course, 3 December 1990 came and went with no sign of the
earthquake, although many schools were dismissed for the day and
large numbers of families living near the fault in southern Illinois
decided to spend the day in other, "safer" parts of the country.

What was it about this information that led to such extreme
behavior? We argue that it was the availability and the vividness of
the information about the prediction that caused many people to
overestimate the likelihood of an earthquake.

Things or events you've encountered more often are usually
easy to remember—they are more "available" in your memory.
But how easily you remember them may have little to do with how
often you've encountered them. It's easier to remember or imagine
a more vivid event. In the following sections, we provide examples
of both of these causes of availability and explore their impact on
how you negotiate.

EASE OF RETRIEVABILITY

Something easy to recall seems more numerous than something
less easy to recall. For example, two groups who heard different
lists of names of well-known personalities were asked whether the
lists contained the names of more men or women. One list had
more men's names, but the women on it were relatively more

famous. The other list had more women's names, but the men listed were relatively more famous. In each case, the groups incorrectly guessed that the lists had more names of the sex of the more famous personalities.[2]

People tend to overestimate the probability of unlikely events if the memories associated with them are particularly vivid and, thus, easier to recall. For instance, if you see a house burning, it increases your belief that such an accident will recur much more than just reading about a house fire in the newspaper. For many Illinois residents, the memory of the San Francisco earthquake of October 1989 and the damage it caused was probably still very vivid, and was refreshed when their newscasters reviewed the event as part of their coverage of the earthquake-prediction story.

Marie Wilson and her colleagues demonstrated the impact of the vividness of information in a study in which two groups of participants, acting as jurors, were shown videotaped closing arguments from a civil trial involving contract claims between a contractor and subcontractor.[3] One taped argument supported the contractor's claim with ten vivid statements; in the other, the contractor's claim was supported by ten dull statements. For example, the more vivid statement, "the slab was jagged and had to be sanded," was substituted by the duller "the slab was rough and had to be planed."

When the jurors passed judgment on the claims and appropriate damages, the contractor prevailed against the subcontractor almost twice as often (82% versus 46%) and was awarded more money when his arguments were vivid. In explaining their decisions, jurors who had seen the vivid presentation could recall more facts about the case than could those who had seen the dull presentation.

In negotiation, managers who present information in colorful or emotionally vivid ways exert a much greater impact on decisions than individuals with equally informative, but dull, presentations. An executive should be aware of the power and influence the control of information—both the amount and the way it's presented—can have on a negotiation's outcome.

ESTABLISHED SEARCH PATTERNS

People have established information search patterns that can make certain types of information more prominent because of the way they are stored in memory. For example, when asked to judge the frequency of words beginning with the letter "r" relative to words that have "r" as the third letter, people overwhelmingly guess that the former are more frequent than the latter.[4] Actually, the opposite is true. The alphabetical structure of memory makes the search for words such as those that begin with the letter "r" easier than the search for words that have "r" as the third letter. In the game of Scrabble, think how much easier it is for you to come up with words that begin with "r" given the seven letters you have to work with than it is to come up with words that have "r" as the third letter.

In another example, when a group of sales, production, accounting, and human resource executives from a large manufacturing company were asked to identify the most important problem facing their company, they each identified the company's problem in terms of their own functional area of expertise. Because their organizational problem-solving experiences and their problem-solving strategies were typically from relatively narrow areas, that is where they searched for the answer. This is hardly surprising. It is unlikely that an accounting executive would be routinely expected to solve production or marketing problems.

While this may be a very efficient way for an executive in a functional area to work, its impracticality is clear when a promotion occurs. If a new company president is selected from production but the problems faced by that company are in marketing, the new president will probably have a hard time solving them with his production-oriented approaches.

AVAILABILITY AND NEGOTIATION

Managers need to insure that the availability of certain information does not overwhelm their ability to analyze a negotiation situation effectively. A careful analysis of alternative proposals, priorities, and the costs associated with each is necessary to know exactly when it is in their best interests to reach agreement.

To negotiate rationally, managers should draw on their past experiences as well as present information to assess various choices. Unfortunately, past experiences aren't likely to be equally accessible in memory. Some experiences will be more available than others. This makes it harder to pay attention to the (objectively) important aspects of a negotiation and to evaluate options without being influenced by the relative availability of certain information. For example, research has shown that employees (who said they valued medical insurance highly) would take an additional $142 a month in salary instead of their insurance benefit. That insurance benefit, to which they contributed $62 a month and their employer $190 a month, had a market value of $340. Because the employees focused on the most available piece of information—their own insurance premium—they significantly underestimated both the market value of the insurance and their employer's contribution.

The task for benefit managers is clear: How can the availability bias be overcome to the extent that employees value their benefits at least at the amount the employer pays?

Employees use the value of their contribution as the anchor to evaluate the worth of this benefit because of its relative availability. While there are many potential anchors on which to base strategy in a negotiation, relative availability is a primary reason some anchors are considered and others ignored.

In a study of collective bargaining and arbitration, we found that the outcomes managers were willing to accept were anchored and influenced by the availability of information about costs.[5] If we emphasized the personal costs of reaching a poor settlement, such as a negative evaluation by the negotiator's constituency, negotiators were less concessionary and more willing to invoke arbitration. When the organizational costs of resorting to arbitration (such as losses in money, time, and control of the outcome) were emphasized, negotiators were significantly more concessionary and more likely to settle.

Consider a negotiation familiar to many—buying a new car. In negotiating the price, you typically discuss the characteristics of the particular make and model you want, including the options available, its reliability, and so forth. Once you agree to a price, the sales person usually tries to sell you a service contract saying, "And for only a couple of dollars more a month, you'll never have to worry about repairs." (An offer made for the car whose major virtue a few minutes ago was its incredible reliability!) Why do nearly half of new car buyers succumb to the pitch and purchase extended warranties?[6]

One reason may be that the buyers believe the extended warranty is a good deal. After all, cars do require repairs—even very reliable cars—and you can probably remember repair bills that cost more than the price of the warranty. The typical $25 deductible seems minor by comparison. So, with the help of the sales person, you can easily imagine the financial burdens of huge repair bills. When your anchor is the thousands of dollars you just committed yourself to spending for the car, a "few additional dollars" seems slight. So, you buy the extended warranty.

But not so fast! There are other things to consider before buying the contract. Almost all extended warranties duplicate the manufacturer's warranties. That is, if your new car has a two-year, twenty-four-thousand mile warranty, and you buy the typical extended warranty of five years and 100,000 miles, what you are really purchasing is an additional three-year, seventy-six-thousand mile warranty. It's clearly in the dealer's interest to sell this to you. Based upon documents filed in a recent lawsuit against Nissan, the typical extended warranty contract costing $795 was mostly pure profit for the dealer. Only $131 went to cover actual repairs; $109 went to Nissan for administrative costs; and the remaining $555 went to the dealer.

CONCLUSIONS

Good negotiation and decision making requires that you identify and use truly reliable, not just available, information. Information that is easily recalled because it is vivid may be interpreted as being reliable when it's not. Unfortunately, it's hard to defuse the impact of availability. While you can set up structures, as we've described, to reduce irrational escalation of commitment, the availability bias is much more subtle. You can only use information that's "available" to you, and information that's easy to recall gets the most attention. You have to distinguish what's emotionally familiar to you from what's reliable and relevant. This *is* complex, but it's necessary if you want to improve the quality of your negotiated agreements.

CHAPTER

7

The Winner's Curse

The famous comedian Groucho Marx said that he didn't want to be a member of any club that would have him as a member. Why? A club's acceptance of his application told him something about its standards—if they were so low as to accept him, he didn't want to join! Most people don't have Groucho's insight, and often make offers in negotiating without realizing the implications of having those offers accepted. Consider the following story:

> You are in a foreign country and meet a merchant who is selling a very attractive gem. You've purchased a few gems in your life, but are far from an expert. After some discussion, you make what you're fairly sure is a low offer. The merchant quickly accepts, and the gem is yours. How do you feel?

Most people would feel uneasy. This is known as the "winner's curse." Yet, why would you voluntarily make an offer that you would not want accepted? Consider the following problem.[1]

ACQUIRING A COMPANY

You represent Company A (the acquirer), which is considering acquiring Company T (the target) by means of a tender offer. You plan to tender in cash for 100 percent of Company T's shares but are unsure how high a price to offer. The main complication is this: the value of Company T depends directly on the outcome of a major oil exploration project it is currently undertaking. Indeed,

Company T's very viability depends on that outcome. If the project fails, the company under current management will be worth nothing. But if the project succeeds, the value of the company under current management could be as high as $100/share. All share values between $0 and $100 are considered equally likely.

By all estimates, the company will be worth considerably more in the hands of Company A than under current management. In fact, whatever the ultimate value under current management, *Company T will be worth fifty percent more under the management of A*. If the project fails, the company is worth $0/share under either management. If the exploration project generates a $50/share value under current management, the value under Company A is $75/share. Similarly, a $100/share value under Company T implies a $150/share value under Company A, and so on.

Company A's board of directors has asked you to determine the price they should offer for Company T's shares. This offer must be made now, *before* the exploration outcome is known. From all indications, Company T would be happy to be acquired by Company A, *provided it is at a profitable price*. Moreover, Company T wishes to avoid, at all cost, the potential of a takeover bid by any other firm. You expect Company T to delay a decision on your bid until the results of the project are in and then accept or reject your offer before the news of the results reaches the press.

Thus, *you (Company A) will not know the results of the exploration project when submitting your price offer, but Company T will know the results when deciding whether or not to accept your offer. In addition, Company T is expected to accept any offer by Company A that is greater than the (per share) value of the company under current management.*

As the representative of Company A, you are deliberating over offers in the range of $0/share (this is tantamount to making no offer at all) to $150/share. What price per share would you tender for Company T's stock?

The "Acquiring a Company" exercise is logically similar to the gem merchant problem, and we believe that Groucho's insight helps to solve both problems. In "Acquiring a Company," you are uncertain about the ultimate value of the target firm. You know only that its value under current management is between $0 and $100, with all values equally likely. Since the firm is expected to be worth 50 percent more under the acquirer's management than under the current ownership, it appears to make sense for a transaction to take place.

The problem is analytically quite simple (as we demonstrate shortly), yet intuitively quite perplexing. The responses of 123 MBA students from Boston University are shown in figure 7.1. Most responses were between $50 and $75. How was this decision reached?

One common, but incorrect, thought process behind the answers shown on figure 7.1 can be paraphrased as follows: "On the average, the firm will be worth $50 to the target and $75 to the acquirer; consequently, a transaction in this range will be profitable to both parties." This logic would be rational if the target firm had the same, incomplete information about its value. However, you knew that the target would know its true value before accepting or rejecting your offer. Now consider the rationale behind deciding whether to make an offer of $60 per share:

> If the acquirer offers $60 per share, the offer will be accepted 60 percent of the time—whenever the target firm is worth between $0 and $60. Since all values are equally likely between $0 and $60 the target will, on average, be worth $30 per share when it accepts a $60 per share offer, and will be worth $45 per share to the acquirer, resulting in a loss of $15 per share. Consequently, a $60 per share offer is unwise.

It's easy to see that the same kind of reasoning applies to *any* offer other than $0. On the average, the acquirer obtains a

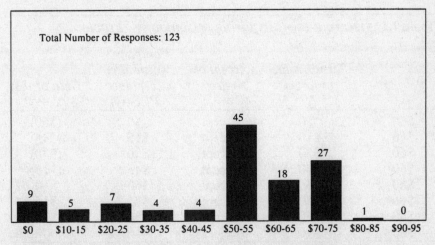

Total Number of Responses: 123

Figure 7.1 Responses in the "Acquiring a Company" Exercise

company worth 25 percent less than the price it pays when the offer is accepted. If the acquirer offers $X (you can substitute your offer for X as we analyze the problem) and the target accepts, the current value of the company is worth anywhere between $0 and $X. As the problem is formulated, any value in that range is equally likely, and the expected value of the offer is therefore equal to $X divided by 2. Since the company is worth 50 percent more to the acquirer, the acquirer's expected value is only 75 percent of its offer. Thus, for any value of $X, the best the acquirer can do is not to make an offer ($0 per share).

It is certainly possible to make money by making an offer on the firm, but you are twice as likely to lose money. See table 7.1 for an illustration. If you were to offer $60/share, the offer would be accepted as long as the value of the firm to the target is $60 or less. You would not make money unless the value is over $40. This series of calculations can be made for any offer. On the average, you lose 25 percent of what you bid.

The paradox of "Acquiring a Company" is that even though the firm is always worth more to the acquirer than to the target, any offer above $0 leads to a negative expected return to the acquirer. *The source of this paradox lies in the high likelihood that the target will accept the acquirer's offer when the firm is least valuable to the acquirer—i.e., when it is a "lemon."*[2]

This answer is so counterintuitive that only 9 of 123 Boston University MBA students correctly offered $0 per share. We've run this experiment with MIT masters candidates, CEOs, CPAs, and

Table 7.1 *Assessing the "Acquiring a Company" Problem*

Offer made (x)	Firm's value to target (y)	Accept or reject	Company's worth after acceptance (1.5x = y)	Gain or loss (x − y)
$60	$0	Accept	$0	($60)
$60	$10	Accept	$15	($45)
$60	$20	Accept	$30	($30)
$60	$30	Accept	$45	($15)
$60	$40	Accept	$60	0
$60	$50	Accept	$75	$15
$60	$60	Accept	$90	$30
$60	$70	Reject	—	—

investment bankers—always with similar results. Even subjects who were paid according to their performance did no better.[3]

While most people have the analytical ability to follow the logic that the optimal offer is $0 per share, most make a positive offer. When making their decisions, they ignore the fact that any outcome is conditional on acceptance by the other party, and that acceptance is most likely to occur when it's least desirable to the person making the offer.

The key feature of the "winner's curse" for negotiating is that one side, usually the seller, often has much better information than the other. Though everyone is familiar with the slogan "buyer beware," it's difficult to put this idea into practice when the other side knows more than you. Against a better informed opponent, your expected return from a transaction decreases dramatically.

APPLICATIONS TO NEGOTIATION

While many readers of "Acquiring a Company" are disappointed that they didn't answer $0, they are often critical of the problem's apparently artificial nature; however, it's easy to find the winner's curse in many real-world contexts. For example:

> Your company transfers you to a new city (or you accept a job with a new firm in a different city) that you don't know well. The real estate market in the new city is favorable to buyers. You wish to avoid moving twice, so you decide to buy a house. While you know very little about the real estate in this new city, a friend has recommended a "very good" real estate agent. After looking at eleven houses in two days, you make an offer on a house. It is immediately accepted. Did you make a good purchase?

You had limited information—you saw ten other houses on the market and accepted advice from the agent whose income goes up if you buy. And you now know that the seller accepted your offer. What do you learn from that fact? Perhaps the house isn't as valuable as you thought. Maybe the seller knows more about the local market and the true condition of the house. Having better information, the seller is most likely to accept your offer when it's higher than the house's true value. Obviously, this logic applies to any situation where one side knows more than the other.

The winner's curse is also found in the used-car market. George Akerlof writes on the market for "lemons": Used cars are expected to vary in their reliability but most buyers cannot tell the difference between more and less reliable used cars. As a result, sellers of less reliable used cars can sell them for the same price as more reliable used cars—a price that doesn't reflect the more reliable cars' true value. Thus, because sellers of better cars can't get a fair price, they are more likely not to sell. As their cars disappear from the market, only the worst used cars are sold—at prices that reflect their quality.[4]

Taken to the extreme, the Akerlof argument predicts fewer used goods for sale than there actually are. The reason for this is that people who buy used goods don't consider the fact that the sellers have selectively chosen to sell them. Thus, many buyers make offers without realizing this information disadvantage, and suffer the winner's curse.

There are ways to avoid the winner's curse. Sellers of high quality or reliable goods (new or used) and services can take steps to reassure buyers about their quality. Car dealers provide customer guarantees. Organizations maintain a reputation so that you can trust their goods or services. Consumers are more likely to stay in a hotel chain in an unfamiliar city because the reputation of the brand name gives them some confidence in the level of service they can expect.

Obviously, an ongoing relationship between parties can also solve or reduce the winner's curse, since a seller may not want to harm the relationship by taking advantage of a buyer. Thus, relatives and friends often buy used cars from each other. Many companies set up bulletin boards where employees can list items for sale, not only to save advertising costs, but also to help the buyer feel confident about the items' true values. Sellers know it costs them if word gets around the company that they knowingly sold a fellow employee a lemon.[5]

Government intervention can also help solve the winner's curse. Some state and local governments have created "lemon laws" in the used-car market to protect buyers and promote trade.

People don't fully realize the true importance of getting accurate information when making transactions. There's great value in a mechanic's unbiased evaluation of a used car, a professional inspector's assessment of a house, or an independent jeweler's assessment of a coveted gem. To protect yourself, you need to develop, borrow, or buy professional expertise to make up for any information you don't have. Many people don't like paying for something (an appraisal) that will probably confirm what they already thought was true. They see this as money for nothing. They would be acting more rationally if they looked at independent appraisals as insurance against buying a lemon, whether it's a car, an overpriced house, or a piece of glass disguising itself as a ruby.

CONCLUSIONS

We've found that managers who take into account the other side's perspective are most successful in negotiation simulations.[6] This focus allows them to better predict the opponent's behavior. Most people have a hard time thinking this way.[7] Overall, *executives in a negotiation tend to act as if their opponent is inactive and ignore the valuable information that can be learned by thinking about the other side's decisions.*

This tendency was also described in the $20 auction in Chapter 2. Why do bidders get involved? Because people see the potential for profit early in the auction and fail to think of what the auction looks like to other bidders. But if you actively think about the other party, you can act more rationally. In "Acquiring a Company," having individuals first play the role of the seller increases the chance they will act rationally when they become the buyer.[8] In a negotiation, if each side understands and can explain the viewpoint of the other, it increases the likelihood of reaching a negotiated resolution.[9]

CHAPTER
8

Overconfidence and Negotiator Behavior

You've seen how a series of biases can reduce the quality of both decision making and outcomes in negotiation. One reason that so many people do poorly in negotiation, that so many are affected by these biases, is the final bias we discuss—overconfidence. Many of the biases, identified earlier can combine to inflate a manager's confidence in his or her judgments and choices, particularly about moderate or difficult issues.[1] In this chapter, we look at the detrimental impact of overconfidence. Consider the attempted buyout of RJR Nabisco by Ross Johnson and his management group:

Disappointed with the stock performance of RJR Nabisco, CEO Ross Johnson decided that a leveraged buyout was the best way to increase shareholder value. In his negotiations with the board of directors' special committee charged to maximize shareholder value, Johnson acted on a series of irrational assumptions. Because of his obvious RJR management connection, he assumed that the deal would go in his favor, that all his investment bankers would have to do would be to set up the financing. He also expected the RJR board of directors to give him the power to manage the deal. Together with Shearson Lehman Hutton, his primary financial partner, Johnson offered an initial buyout price of $75/share.[2] This offer required the management team to put up only $20 million or 8.5 percent of the deal. If the offer were accepted, they would receive over 18 percent of the firm's equity. Though Johnson insisted that this equity was to be divided among the fifteen thousand RJR workers, only six names emerged as beneficiaries of this transaction. In fact, the deal that Johnson was proposing led the *New York Times* to label him the "robber baron."

Johnson and his management group were so overconfident in their ability to close this deal that they disregarded many warnings from the board of directors and made no significant concessions to them. In addition, they didn't seriously consider or plan for the entry of other major bidders for RJR Nabisco. Johnson assumed that, as the top bidder, he would be able to buy the company, but he lost the deal to Kohlberg, Kravis, and Roberts (KKR), an investment banking firm specializing in leveraged buyouts, even though his final per share price was higher than the $109 winning bid offered by KKR. Johnson had so prejudiced the board against him that they chose KKR. KKR's flexibility in the negotiation and their concern for RJR's future success was preferable to Johnson's arrogance and overconfidence.

Johnson's overconfidence in his judgments is not unique to him or other managers. It's a bias with which everyone must contend when making complex judgments. Before we continue our discussion of overconfidence, take a few minutes to complete the following quiz.

Listed below are ten requests for information you are unlikely to know. For each write down your best estimate of the answer. Then put a lower and upper bound around your estimate such that you are 95 percent confident that the correct answer falls within this "confidence range."

_____ a. Number of General Motors automobiles produced in 1990

_____ b. IBM's assets in 1989

_____ c. Total number of $5 bills in circulation on 31 March 1990

_____ d. Total area in square miles of Lake Michigan

_____ e. Total population of Barcelona, Spain, in 1990

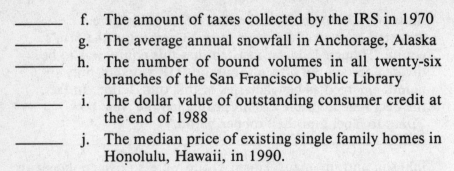

_____ f. The amount of taxes collected by the IRS in 1970

_____ g. The average annual snowfall in Anchorage, Alaska

_____ h. The number of bound volumes in all twenty-six branches of the San Francisco Public Library

_____ i. The dollar value of outstanding consumer credit at the end of 1988

_____ j. The median price of existing single family homes in Honolulu, Hawaii, in 1990.

How many of your ten ranges actually include the correct answers? If you set your ranges so that you are 95 percent confident, nine or ten of them should. The correct answers for each of these items are: (a) 3,213,752; (b) $77,734,000,000; (c) 5,772,195,480; (d) 67,900 square miles; (e) 4,163,000 people; (f) $195,722,096,497; (g) 68.5 inches; (h) 1,749,129; (i) $728,900,000,000; and (j) $290,400.

If these answers fell within nine or ten of your ranges, we could conclude that you were appropriately confident in your estimation ability. However, most people's ranges only surround between thirty and seventy percent of the correct answers, despite their claiming 95 percent confidence. Why? Most people are overconfident concerning their estimating abilities and don't acknowledge that uncertainty exists.

Consider the following, more applied scenario.

You are an adviser to a major-league baseball player. In baseball, when a player and a team owner don't agree on compensation, they submit final offers to an arbitrator. The arbitrator must accept one position or the other, not a compromise. The challenge for each side is to come just a little closer to the arbitrator's perception of the appropriate compensation package than the other. In this case, your best estimate of the final offer that the team owner will submit is a package worth $300,000 per year. You believe that an appropriate wage is $500,000 per year but estimate the arbitrator's opinion to be $400,000 per year. What final offer do you propose?

This scenario sets up a common trap for managers. Because people are overconfident that their judgments are correct, they are also likely to be overconfident in their estimate of a neutral party's opinion and the chances that he or she will agree with their position. In the baseball example, if the arbitrator's true assessment of the appropriate wage is $400,000 and you think the wage should be $500,000, you are likely to submit an inappropriately high offer and overestimate the likelihood of its acceptance. Consequently, this overconfidence is likely to lead you, as the adviser, to think less compromise is necessary than a more objective analysis would suggest. In fact, agents and team owners are often guilty of exactly this bias.

In a study of negotiator behavior,[3] we asked negotiators who were participating in final-offer arbitration to estimate the probability that the offer they submitted would be accepted as the binding contract. As in the baseball example, the arbitrator was limited to accepting only one side's offer, without any compromises. Thus, the *average* probability that any one offer would be accepted by the arbitrator had to be 50 percent (one of the two offers had to be accepted). However, the negotiators, on average, reported that their final offers had a 68 percent chance of being accepted. While any one offer might have a 68 percent chance of being accepted, its compliment could only have a 32 percent chance of acceptance—the percentages, objectively, have to average to 50 percent. These negotiators were overconfident. They reported that their offers were 18 percent more likely to be accepted than they could be.

Overconfidence may inhibit a variety of possible, and acceptable, settlements. When a manager is overconfident that his or her particular position will be accepted, it reduces the incentive to compromise. However, with a more accurate assessment, an executive is likely to be more uncertain about the probability of success and more willing to propose and/or accept a compromise.

We demonstrated this effect in a study on the impact of training on negotiator overconfidence. After training a group of negotiators on the overconfidence bias, we found that negotiators without the training assigned higher probabilities of success to their positions (vis-à-vis the arbitrator's choice) and were significantly less likely to compromise and reach agreement (prior to arbitration) than were the negotiators we had trained.[4]

In addition to training, considering the suggestions of qualified advisers is another way to temper overconfidence. However, there are many situations in which you must negotiate without benefit of counsel. In these situations, you must rely on other ways to avoid overconfidence. A successful strategy is to ask people to explain why their decisions might be wrong (or considerably off the mark); this strategy works by getting individuals to see the obvious problems in their judgments.[5] Finally, everyone should be reminded that overconfidence is most likely to occur when your knowledge is limited.

It's also helpful to seek objective assessments about a position from a *neutral* party. You're likely to get an assessment that is much closer to the other side's position than you might intuitively predict, which should help to reduce any overconfidence you may have in the "correctness" of your position.

THE PERVASIVENESS OF OVERCONFIDENCE

While training can help, overconfidence has proved difficult to eradicate completely. One reason may be that other factors or biases seem to work together to enhance the overconfidence with which managers evaluate their judgments. We look at these other biases in this section.

ANCHORING

Tversky and Kahneman explain overconfidence in terms of anchoring.[6] They argue that when individuals are asked to set a confidence range around an answer or judgment, their initial estimate serves as an anchor that biases the range they set. Because people usually make insufficient adjustments from an anchor, the confidence range is overly narrow.

THE WINNER'S CURSE

In the winner's curse, an executive has less information than his or her opponent. As we discussed in the last chapter, one factor that leads to the winner's curse is when the executive ignores the other side's perspective. This tends to encourage overconfidence, as demonstrated in the twenty-dollar-bill auction in Chapter 2. The only way participants can justify entering the auction is to consider the situation only from their perspective. Otherwise, it quickly becomes obvious that entering is irrational.

NEED-BASED ILLUSIONS

People distort their perceptions of situations to make themselves feel more competent and secure. These distortions result in "need-based illusions." Like the other biases discussed, need-based illusions lead to irrational behavior. Unlike those biases, however, need-based illusions are motivational. They make a situation seem more palatable, while influencing your decision making and negotiation.[7]

There are three well-documented need-based illusions: illusion of superiority, illusion of optimism, and illusion of control.[8] The illusion of superiority is based upon an unrealistically positive view of the self. People believe that, on the average, they are more honest, capable, intelligent, courteous, insightful, and fair than others. They give themselves more responsibility for their own successes and take less responsibility for their own failures, but they hold other people responsible when they fail and don't give them credit when they succeed.[9] Psychologist Rod Kramer and his colleagues have found that negotiators are especially likely to believe that they are more flexible, purposeful, competent, fair, honest, and cooperative than their opponents.[10]

The illusion of optimism means that, in general, people underestimate their chances of experiencing "bad" future events and overestimate the likelihood that they will experience "good" future events.

The illusion of control means that people believe they have more control over outcomes than they really do, even in such obviously random events as throwing dice.[11] One instance of this is the curious discovery that people are willing to bet significantly larger amounts of money on the races that haven't yet run than on races that have already run, but whose results are unknown. They believe their betting on a race will influence its outcome.

These need-based illusions lead people to see the world not as it is, but as they would like it to be. As a result, managers are often more secure in their judgments and more confident in the "correctness" of their choices than they should be.

SEARCHING FOR CONFIRMING EVIDENCE

As we pointed out earlier, when people hold certain beliefs or expectations, they tend to ignore information that contradicts them. Consider the following problem we've given to our classes.[12]

> Here is a three-number sequence: 2–4–6. Your task is to discover the numeric rule that produced these numbers. To determine the rule, you can generate other sets of three numbers that we will acknowledge as either conforming or not conforming to the actual rule. You can stop producing sets of three numbers when you think you've discovered the rule. How would you go about this task?

In our classes, the first response is usually to propose sets of numbers such as 4–6–8 and 10–12–14, using an "ascending even numbers" rule. While our rule would also produce these two sets of numbers, their proposed rule is not ours. Then class members often propose numbers such as 5–10–15 and 100–200–300, the rule being "the difference between the first two numbers equals the difference between the last two numbers." Again, the class has come up with the wrong rule.

The actual rule we used is "any three ascending numbers"—a solution that required the accumulation of *disconfirming,* rather than confirming, evidence. To discover how the true rule differs from your hypothesized rule, you must try sequences that do *not* conform to your rule. Trying the sequences 1–2–3, 10–15–20, 122–126–130, and so forth will only lead you into the confirmation trap. Finding the correct rule often requires a willingness to disprove your initial beliefs or hypotheses.

Managers don't often seek to disprove an initial belief. Charles Lord, Lee Ross, and Mark Lepper selected participants for a study based upon their support for or opposition to capital punishment.[13] The subjects were presented with two (purportedly) authentic empirical studies. One supported their position; the other opposed their position. While they read these two studies, the participants were asked several times to evaluate their quality. Both the proponents and opponents of capital punishment rated the study that supported their beliefs as more convincing and better-conducted than one that opposed their beliefs. Further, the net effect of reading these two studies was to polarize further each group's beliefs. It seems that people are more likely to take at face value information they agree with and scrutinize more carefully information they don't.

Managers tend to enter negotiations with one strategy for reaching agreement. They assume success and develop their strategy accordingly. A very different view, and one we believe is more useful, is to realize that your initial strategy may not work and seek to disconfirm it by searching for new information. If you are not open to disconfirming information, you will have a harder time adapting when confronted by unexpected circumstances in a negotiation.

CAMPEAU-FEDERATED MERGER RECONSIDERED

In the second chapter, we suggested that the Campeau-Federated merger failed because of Robert Campeau's irrational escalation of his commitment to acquire Federated Department Stores. It's likely that there were multiple biases at work that also contributed to his failure.

Campeau, extraordinarily successful in the real estate market, probably anchored on his past success, part of which was his willingness to go against prevailing wisdom. If Campeau had succeeded he would have been considered a maverick, but because he failed he was criticized (luck has a lot to do with how one's decision-making ability is perceived). His illusions of control and optimism also probably added to his overconfidence; he was successful in the past, he would be successful again.

Once the need-based illusions took hold, Campeau's overconfidence was fed by information he found that confirmed his expectations about turning this merger into a very profitable venture. Any information that indicated he was overestimating Federated's potential was likely ignored.

Finally, he clearly ignored the information and perspective of the other bidder—Macy's. Given that the executives at Macy's were probably considerably more knowledgeable about the retail business than Campeau, their involvement signaled that a takeover was probably advantageous. However, they were also better able to evaluate the worth of Federated Department Stores and know when to get out of the bidding.

Thus, Campeau was a victim of a series of biases that reduced his ability to reach a good, high-quality negotiated outcome. Any manager can sabotage him or herself in the same way. In the next section, we add to this perspective with a detailed examination of the two major strategic perspectives on negotiation: integrative and distributive bargaining.

TWO

A Rational Framework for Negotiation

CHAPTER
9

Thinking Rationally about Negotiation

In the first section of this book, we described how and why managers can make irrational decisions in a negotiation. Now we look at how managers *should* make decisions in a world where many people don't always behave rationally. To negotiate rationally, you must understand what makes you sometimes think irrationally, while anticipating similar irrationality from your opponents.

In this chapter we examine the two critical components of a rational negotiation process. First, an effective manager must objectively evaluate each party's alternatives to a negotiated agreement, interests, and priorities. Together, these three sets of information determine a negotiation's structure.[1] Second, an effective manager must understand the integrative and distributive components of negotiation, in order to enlarge the pie of available resources and increase his or her share.[2] We also draw upon the information from the first section of the book to outline prescriptions to prevent you from making the common mistakes that interfere with the development of a rational negotiation strategy.

INFORMATION TO ASSESS IN A NEGOTIATION

ALTERNATIVES TO A NEGOTIATED AGREEMENT

Before you begin any important negotiation, you should consider the potential consequences of failing to reach an agreement. You need to determine your *Best Alternative To a Negotiated Agreement* (BATNA).[3] This is critical because your BATNA determines the lowest value acceptable to you for a negotiated agreement; if the parties cannot reach agreement, they settle for their BATNAs. Thus, any agreement that is of higher value than your BATNA is better than an impasse.

Most people enter into negotiations with a general target or at least some idea of what they want; however, many executives don't specifically establish their own or their opponent's *reservation price.* A reservation price is the point at which you are indifferent to whether a negotiation reaches agreement or ends in an impasse. It's closely related to your BATNA. For example, rather than buying a new car from a particular dealer, one alternative you could consider is to use mass transit. Alternatively, your BATNA could be to buy the same car from another dealer, with your reservation price being the price offered by the second dealer. While it's easier to assess the value to you of the second price offered than to put a "price" on using mass transit, it's critical in either situation to determine the value of your BATNA. By thinking about your BATNA, you can rationally assess the highest price you are willing to pay before you would prefer an impasse. If you make an offer near your reservation price and it's rejected, you know that any further concession to reach an agreement is unacceptable to you. *Remember the goal of negotiating is not to reach just any agreement, but to reach an agreement that is better for you than what you would get without one.*

While it may seem obvious that you should know your alternatives when negotiating, most people don't take this rational step. One common example of this is an event we have come to refer to as the Sunday night real-estate call. Since many open houses are held on Sundays, negotiation instructors often receive telephone calls on Sunday nights from friends, friends of friends, friends of relatives, etc., that sound something like this:

Hello, Maggie. You don't know me, but we have a mutual friend—Sarah. I looked at a house this afternoon, and was telling Sarah about it. The house is absolutely wonderful. I love it! The asking price was $249,000. The kitchen has really interesting wooden cabinets . . . (fifteen minute of needless detail on the house) . . . Anyway, I offered $222,000 earlier this evening, and they countered at $237,000. I was telling Sarah about this, and she suggested that I call you to figure out what I should do next. What do you recommend?

We don't like getting these calls. They are no-win situations for us. If our advice leads to a higher price than the caller had hoped, he or she is unimpressed with our expertise. If our advice leads to losing the house to another buyer, the caller will be angry at us—especially since the house is so wonderful. Unfortunately, getting the lowest possible price often requires running the risk of losing the house to another buyer. In fact, any strategy other than accepting the other party's offer means some risk of impasse.

So what advice can we give our caller? We say that he or she has already violated the most important rule of buying houses (or making any other important exchange, with the possible exception of mate selection): "Fall in love with three, not with one." To make a well-informed decision, a buyer must first think about what would happen if he or she did not buy the house. How attractive is the next best option? To the extent that the buyer loves *only* this house and has to have it, any bargaining position is weakened.

Falling in love with one house (or car, or company) prevents you from thinking clearly and rationally about your best alternative and compromises your competitive edge in the negotiation. If you have an alternative, you are better able to risk losing the first house by waiting for the other party to make a concession. An alternative strengthens your position.

Prescription 1: Assess what you will do if you don't reach an agreement with your current negotiation opponent.

While executives rarely think rationally about their own alternatives to a negotiated agreement, we noted in Chapter 7 that it is even rarer for them to think about their opponent's decisions and alternatives. However, by considering the other party's circumstances and likely alternatives to an agreement, you can get a wealth of information about how far they will move before actually walking away from the negotiating table. For example, the seller of a house who has already purchased another one will act very differently than a seller who is just testing the residential market. Knowing this can give a potential buyer a distinct advantage.

Unfortunately, it can be difficult to assess the other party's alternatives. Despite this, managers should always know their own

BATNA and make their best estimates of an opponent's BATNA.

Prescription 2: Assess what your current negotiation opponent will do if they do not reach an agreement with you.

THE INTERESTS OF THE PARTIES

A complete analysis of a negotiation includes identifying the interests of all parties. Roger Fisher and Bill Ury emphasized the importance of distinguishing between underlying interests and positions.[4] A position is the stated requirement that one side demands from the other. An interest is what each side really desires, even if it is not publicly stated. Sometimes focusing on interests helps identify more useful solutions. Consider the following example:[5]

Prior to the Camp David agreement between Israel and Egypt, both parties described their interests as ownership over the Sinai. In trying to negotiate the control of the Sinai Peninsula, it appeared that the two sides had directly opposing goals. Egypt wanted the return of the Sinai in its entirety, while Israel, which had occupied the territory since the 1967 war, refused. Efforts at compromise failed; neither side found the proposal of splitting the Sinai acceptable. Therefore, a solution wasn't possible if the negotiation remained focused on the stated positions of each side, namely control over the Sinai.

However, the negotiation was resolved when both parties gained a better understanding of their underlying interests: land ownership for Egypt and military security for Israel.

Prescription 3: Assess the true issues in the negotiation.

THE RELATIVE IMPORTANCE OF EACH PARTY'S INTERESTS

While managers often have several interests in a negotiation, they rarely evaluate the relative importance of each. To be fully prepared to negotiate, you must clearly identify your priorities. Effective trade-offs can then be accomplished by conceding less important issues to gain on more important issues. In the Israel-Egypt dispute, Egypt cared more about ownership of the land, while Israel cared more about the security that the land provided. The solution at Camp David that emerged traded off these two principal issues: Israel returned the Sinai to Egypt in exchange for assurances of a demilitarized zone and new Israeli air bases.

Prescription 4: Assess how important each issue is to you.

Although you may often find you don't have enough information to assess your opponent's true preferences, it's important to recognize this deficiency. It helps clarify what you need to learn during the negotiation. As each party tries to persuade the other, you can learn many critical pieces of information. Too often, the negotiation isn't used as an opportunity to improve the quality and quantity of information you have about the opposition. Knowing what information you're missing keeps you from making the errors described earlier. It is far better to realize that the other side has some valuable information that you don't know than to make uninformed assumptions.

Alternatives, interests, and their relative importance provide the building blocks for analyzing the distributive and integrative aspects of a negotiation. Assessing this information before entering any important negotiation prepares you to analyze the two primary tasks of negotiation: integration, or the enlargement of the pie of available resources, and distribution, the claiming of the pie.[6] Richard Walton and Robert McKersie first suggested the critical need to think simultaneously about these two dimensions of the negotiation problem in the context of labor relations, and much of the analysis in this chapter is an application and extension of their earlier work.[7]

Prescription 5: Assess how important each issue is to your opponent.

THE DISTRIBUTIVE AND INTEGRATIVE DIMENSIONS OF NEGOTIATION

THE DISTRIBUTIVE DIMENSION OF NEGOTIATION AND THE BARGAINING ZONE

All negotiation involves the distribution of outcomes. A single-issue negotiation is purely distributive. One party's gain is the other party's loss. Consider a case in which Company Y (the buyer) is interested in acquiring Company X (the seller). What Company X doesn't know is that while Company Y would like to buy Company X for $18 million, it considers Company X to be worth $30 million (the value of Company Y's BATNA) and would rather pay any price under $30 million than lose the opportunity. What Company Y doesn't know is that while Company X would like to sell the firm to Company Y for $35 million, Company X would rather sell the firm at any price above $20 million (the value of Company X's BATNA) than keep it.

Ben Franklin spoke to this issue: "Trades would not take place unless it were advantageous to the parties concerned. Of course, it is better to strike as good a bargain as one's bargaining position permits. The worst outcome is when, by overreaching greed, no bargain is struck, and a trade that could have been advantageous to both parties does not come off at all."[8] On the other hand, if the sale is to take place, the seller would prefer the highest and the buyer the lowest price possible. The challenge is to identify where the two price ranges overlap, if at all.

During the discussions that follow this case, we are often asked by our students whether it is better to be tough or soft in the negotiation. Suppose a typical soft negotiator sells the target company for $22 million. He or she can at least claim to have gotten a better outcome than those who didn't reach agreement. The typical tough negotiator, who sells Company X for $28 million, will argue that the only way to succeed is to take a tough stand. (Notice that this only works against a soft Company Y negotiator who is willing to pay the $28 million.) Then there are those who reached an impasse. Why didn't they find the $10 million of joint gain possible by reaching an agreement? Why didn't they listen to Ben Franklin's advice? When both parties adopt a tough strategy and assume that the other will cave in, confident that only the tough survive, the result is usually an impasse.

So, is it better to be tough or soft? We propose that it's better to be rational. There are times to be tough and there are times to be soft; the rational manager evaluates each negotiation and creates a strategy that fits the particular context. There is no one-size-fits-all strategy that will guarantee success. Think about your BATNA *and* your opponent's BATNA, and make your best assessment of the *bargaining zone,* the range of settlements within which it's better for both parties to agree than not to agree. The bargaining zone for the transfer of Company X can be diagrammed as follows:

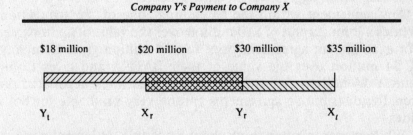

Company Y's Payment to Company X

$18 million $20 million $30 million $35 million

Y_t X_r Y_r X_t

Y_t = Company Y's target price, the price it would be happy to pay: $18 million

X_r = Company X's reservation price, at which Company X is indifferent between keeping or selling the company: $20 million

Y_r = Company Y's reservation price, at which Company Y is indifferent between buying or not buying the company: $30 million

X_t = Company X's target price, the price it would be happy to accept: $35 million

The bargaining zone framework organizes the distributive aspect of a negotiation by showing the overlap, if any, of each side's acceptable price ranges. In the diagram above, the endpoints of this zone are the two reservation prices. Thus, there is a set of agreements that both parties prefer over impasse, which in this case consists of all values between $20 million and $30 million. When the reservation prices of two parties overlap, both parties can benefit by reaching agreement. Conversely, when the reservation prices don't overlap, there is a negative bargaining zone and no settlement that will be acceptable to both parties.

If Company Y could convince Company X that an offer of $21

million was final, Company X would probably accept it. Similarly, if Company X could convince Company Y that $29 million was the lowest amount they would agree to, Company Y would probably accept.

One of the critical pieces of information in a negotiation is the other party's reservation price. If one side can discover the other's reservation price without revealing their own, they can push for a resolution that is only marginally acceptable to the other side. Extreme demands won't work if they are worse than the other side's BATNA. For example, Company X will not accept $15 million, regardless of Company Y's persuasiveness. In order to be tough, a manager must first know the bargaining zone. Knowing your opponent's BATNA allows you to determine whether an offer is conservative, aggressive, or unreasonable.

Any agreement within the bargaining zone of the acquisition creates a joint surplus of $10 million over the value of an impasse. For example, an agreement price of $24 million gives Company X $4 million over the value of their BATNA and gives Company Y $6 million over their BATNA. Thus, when negotiated rationally, distributive agreements can be very profitable for both sides.

While managers often think about a possible settlement price in advance of negotiating, they usually spend too much time thinking about a target price and not enough thinking about the reservation prices and the bargaining zone. It does you no good to demand a price that the other side won't pay. Focus instead on the maximum price they are willing to pay.

Prescription 6: Assess the bargaining zone.

THE INTEGRATIVE DIMENSION OF NEGOTIATION

Sometimes a more careful assessment of each side's relative preferences or interests can produce more joint profit than a purely distributive agreement can. This is the basis of integrative negotiation. In Chapter 3, we argued that there is a mind-set we call the mythical fixed-pie that prevents people from making favorable trade-offs. We discussed examples where this attitude destroyed negotiations that could have been mutually profitable. Understanding the underlying issues of a negotiation and their relative importance for both parties allows you to avoid the mythical fixed-pie and make beneficial trade-offs across issues.

This is illustrated in a story told by Mary Parker Follet.[9] Two sisters both wanted a single orange. A compromise, dividing the orange equally, would leave each sister with only half. By trading the rind for the juice, however, one sister got all of the juice she wanted to drink, and the other sister got the rind to bake a cake.

In this very fortunate trade, both parties were able to get exactly what they wanted. This is rarely the case. More commonly, each side gives up something they care less about for something they care more about. But if you have a clear understanding of each side's interests and their importance, your negotiations can be both successful and rational.

Integrative agreements have a number of important benefits. First, they create better agreements than purely distributive ones. Second, in cases such as the Camp David example, no agreement is possible without finding an integrative agreement. Third, the problem-solving atmosphere of integrative negotiations—finding mutually beneficial trade-offs—and the higher quality agreements that result strengthen the bargaining relationship. But, while the benefits of integrative agreements are clear, managers often fail to find them. As soon as multiple issues surface in a negotiation, look for trade-off opportunities and ways to expand the pie of available resources.

Prescription 7: Assess where the trade-offs exist.

BARRIERS TO RATIONAL NEGOTIATIONS—THE SOLUTION OF ANTICIPATION

This chapter begins to outline a framework for managers to use in thinking about negotiation. It shows that by rationally identifying all the issues and each party's relative concerns for these issues and by rationally thinking about the bargaining zone, you can better increase the size of the bargaining pie *and* your share of it. But the prescriptions in this chapter assume that you will follow rational negotiation advice. Remember the biases we discussed in Chapters 2 to 8 that reduce your ability to act rationally. We encourage you to do a "judgment audit" to ensure that the irrational effects of these biases do not interfere with the framework outlined here. Before making a key decision in a negotiation, ask yourself whether it makes sense or whether you are simply trying to justify an earlier decision (and irrationally escalating your commitment to a previous course of action). Repeat this process with each of the other six biases.

Prescription 8: Assess the degree to which you might be affected by (a) the tendency to irrationally escalate commitment to a previously chosen strategy, (b) the mythical fixed-pie, (c) anchoring and adjustment, (d) the framing of the negotiation, (e) the availability of information, (f) the winner's curse, and (g) overconfidence.

Many of the prescriptions in this chapter require you to focus on the decisions of the other party. This means that you should also accurately assess the biases that may affect your opponent. By thinking realistically about the other party, you can better anticipate and respond to their negotiation decisions.

Prescription 9: Assess the degree to which your negotiation opponent might be affected by (a) the tendency to irrationally escalate commitment to a previously chosen strategy, (b) the mythical fixed-pie, (c) anchoring and adjustment, (d) the framing of the negotiation, (e) the availability of information, (f) the winner's curse, and (g) overconfidence.

Coupling this audit of your and your opponent's decision biases with the prescriptions that follow in the next two chapters will go a long way toward achieving rational outcomes.

CHAPTER
10

Negotiations in a Joint Venture
A Case Example

In this chapter we illustrate the process of rational thinking by analyzing a negotiation case using the prescriptions provided in Chapter 9. We will look at both the distributive and integrative aspects of the negotiation and point out many of the mistakes you want to avoid.

CASE: MANNx-OTC—THE NEW ANALGESIC

You are the executive vice-president of Northcraft and Northcraft (NN), one of the nation's leading pharmaceutical companies. Your firm is a leader in over-the-counter (OTC) products (nonprescription medications). You also have a significantly smaller division that manufactures ethical pharmaceuticals (prescription medications). One of your weaknesses is that you lack a large volume presence in the vast OTC analgesic market, which is currently dominated by three product categories: aspirin-related products, acetaminophen-related (Tylenol) products, and ibuprofen-related (Motrin) products. Your analysts heard recently that a reduced-strength version of the prescription drug betaMANNx, sold by Thompson and Company, was approved by the Food and Drug

Administration for over-the-counter sales. You believe that your marketing department can create an OTC product category for the drug that will make it competitive with the other OTC pain-killers.

Thompson is a high-quality company, but has little capability for reaching a mass market with an OTC product. Historically, Thompson hasn't sold the rights to their products to other firms because they take great pride in their research and development successes as well as their professional image. Your goal is to assess the potential for a successful OTC product joint venture with Thompson that will benefit both firms.

Prescription 1: Assess what you will do if you don't reach an agreement with your current negotiation opponent.

It is critical to know what you will do if you aren't allowed access to betaMANNx. You study this issue and decide you will stay out of the OTC painkiller market for the foreseeable future. Thus, any involvement with Thompson can be judged on your estimate of the bottom-line profitability of this new product. Your analysts predict you can expect a $30 million net profit over the remaining six-year period in which Thompson maintains exclu-sive manufacturing rights to betaMANNx products.[1] After Thompson's patent expires, any firm can produce and market betaMANNx products, dramatically reducing their profitability for all companies.

Prescription 2: Assess what your current negotiation opponent will do if they do not reach an agreement with you.

Your analysts estimate that $12 million is the likely profitability of betaMANNx to Thompson if it remains exclusively a prescrip-tion drug. You don't expect Thompson to enter a joint venture with any other firm. Thus, there seems to be some synergy available to you both in combining their product with your OTC marketing capability, although your analysts realize they need much more data to make an accurate assessment. However, Thompson and Company has agreed to meet with you to discuss the possibility of a joint venture.

Prescription 3: Assess the true issues in the negotiation.

While the most obvious issue in this case is how to share the profits from MANNx-OTC (the over-the-counter version of beta-MANNx), further thought leads to other important issues, such as Thompson's desire to keep betaMANNx on the market as a prescription drug. You expect that the length of time they continue to market it actively is open to discussion. Active marketing means their sales force and promotions are vigorously encouraging doctors to prescribe betaMANNx. Without such marketing efforts, their sales will drop. From your perspective, however, every prescription filled for betaMANNx is one less potential customer for MANNx-OTC. Therefore, the continued marketing of beta-MANNx takes away from MANNx-OTC's profit.

Prescription 4: Assess how important each issue is to you.

Restrictions on Thompson's active marketing of betaMANNx also affect MANNx-OTC's profitability. If betaMANNx is actively marketed, MANNx-OTC will be less attractive to pharmacists, who have many profitable products vying for their limited OTC shelf space. This direct competition between betaMANNx and MANNx-OTC is estimated to reduce the $30 million profit by $2 million for every year (up to six years) that Thompson actively markets the drug.

Prescription 5: Assess how important each issue is to your opponent.

Realizing that Thompson may want to continue marketing betaMANNx, a key issue in the negotiation is to discover the opportunity costs to Thompson of this decision. Finding out such information is often challenging; we discuss this in greater detail in Chapter 11. For now, assume that Thompson and Company has told you in earlier discussions that:

Sales of MANNx-OTC will not hurt our prescription business as long as we are free to continue our active marketing of betaMANNx, which is central to our image as a leading pharmaceutical company. We don't expect to have a product to equal betaMANNx's success for at least two more years so it's important to us to be able to market betaMANNx for the remaining life of the patent. The cost to us of not being able to market betaMANNx is $4 million for the first year, $2.5 million for the second year, $1 million for the third year, and $500,000 for every year thereafter. Thus, failing to market this product for the six remaining years of the patent would reduce our profitability by an estimated $9 million.

With this assessment about the alternatives available and relative value of the issues to you and to Thompson, you are well equipped to begin your distributive and integrative analysis of this situation.

THE DISTRIBUTIVE DIMENSION

Prescription 6: Assess the bargaining zone.

In order to simplify matters, assume that you are negotiating over a joint venture that includes the provision that Thompson will immediately stop their active marketing of betaMANNx. (We soon return to this assumption.) The division of the $30 million profit is estimated by the bargaining zone illustrated in the following diagram.

It is important to remember that both parties may be overly optimistic (see Chapter 8) about what they can get out of the negotiation. While you might want Thompson to accept one-sixth of the profit, this is an unrealistic offer—they can do better by not producing MANNx-OTC. You must also realize that Thompson may also have an unrealistic target price, and you must prevent them from anchoring on it.

You can think of this more rationally by looking at the reservation prices. There are a set of agreements that you both prefer over impasse (i.e., all points between $9 million and $30 million). This large and positive bargaining zone shows you can both gain a great deal by reaching agreement. If your assessment is accurate and you convince Thompson that an offer of $10 million is the most you will give, they will probably accept. However, it's also true that if Thompson can convince you that $25 million is the lowest amount

The Portion of the $30 Million That Thompson Will Receive

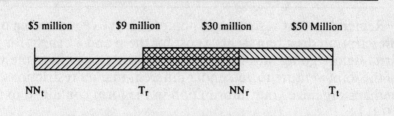

NN$_t$ = NN's target price. You would be delighted to give Thompson and Company $5 million (or 1/6) of the profit from the joint venture.

T$_r$ = Thompson's reservation price. It will cost them $9 million in lost income to give up their active marketing of betaMANNx. Thus, they won't enter a joint venture if they don't receive this level of benefit.

NN$_r$ = NN's reservation point. The product is worth $30 million to you. You wouldn't pay Thompson more than this, and any amount less than this is expected profit.

T$_t$ = Thompson's target price. A high price they would love to receive (they may have little idea of the true potential of MANNx-OTC).

they will accept, you will probably agree. A profit of $5 million is better than no agreement at all.

You can conclude from this distributive analysis that there is a wide range of settlements that make you both better off than an impasse. Yet, even in such cases, impasses do occur. Thinking rationally about the distributive dimension of this case, however, increases your chances of reaching a beneficial agreement. Thinking rationally about the bargaining zone increases your ability to get the most for your side.

THE INTEGRATIVE DIMENSION OF THIS CASE

The preceding section limited the negotiation to only one issue—the exchange of money for the rights to market and sell MANNx-OTC. By definition, single-issue negotiations are distributive. Adding additional issues can increase the amount of total benefit available to both sides by capitalizing on different interests. Looking for novel alternatives, which usually emerge through creative problem solving, can lead to integrative agreements, which increase the size of the pie available to everyone.[2]

Prescription 7: Assess where the trade-offs exist.

Remember that restricting Thompson's active marketing of the prescription drug represents a cost for them and a benefit for your firm. Before going into the negotiation, you can explore the value of the joint venture to you under different market restrictions, and perhaps organize your information in the form contained in table 10.1.

The first outcome, no agreement, has a payoff of $0. The second shows that if you created a joint venture with Thompson ending all active marketing of betaMANNx immediately, it would create

---

Table 10.1 *Northcraft and Northcraft's Payoff Table (in millions)*

Outcome	Lifetime Expected Profit to NN
No joint venture	$0
Joint venture: Thompson stops active marketing of betaMANNx immediately	$30-P
Joint venture: Thompson stops active marketing of betaMANNx after 1 year	$28-P
Joint venture: Thompson stops active marketing of betaMANNx after 2 years	$26-P
Joint venture: Thompson stops active marketing of betaMANNx after 3 years	$24-P
Joint venture: Thompson stops active marketing of betaMANNx after 4 years	$22-P
Joint venture: Thompson stops active marketing of betaMANNx after 5 years	$20-P
Joint venture: Thompson continues active marketing of betaMANNx throughout the product's remaining 6-year life	$18-P

NOTE: P is transfer price NN pays to Thompson for the rights to market and sell MANNx-OTC.

a profit of $30 million. Your company would receive this amount *less* the amount of money Thompson receives for transferring the rights to sell and market MANNx-OTC to your firm, also known as the *transfer price* (P). The alternative solutions involve reducing the restrictions on Thompson's marketing of betaMANNx. For example, if Thompson stops their active marketing after three more years, the profit is reduced to $24 million.

Many managers aren't accustomed to having a complete quantitative assessment of all issues in a negotiation; however, to be effective, you must be able to compare potential trade-offs across issues. One way to do this is to establish your own personal system for evaluating and quantifying a negotiation's different issues and potential outcomes. Such a formula will provide you with an efficient way to compare different issues and allow you to make trade-offs that maximize your priorities.

Using Thompson's marketing information, we estimated the value to them of different settlements at table 10.2. This provides a number of useful insights. First, Thompson can make $12 million on their own; they are unlikely to accept any agreement that gives them less. Second, it's clear that it's more important for them to actively market betaMANNx in the earliest years remaining in the patent. This information, and the fact that their marketing is a constant cost to you, points to a possible trade-off.

Table 10.3 combines the profit assessments from NN and Thompson. It allows you to look at how the two underlying issues of transfer price and the time period for Thompson's active marketing collectively affect the available joint benefit. This value is equal to the difference between the total profits (NN + T) generated by each of the proposed agreements and no agreement at all. For example, $21 million ($33 million less $12 million) is the benefit created by the joint venture when Thompson is not allowed to market betaMANNx. This is the same size as the bargaining zone as identified earlier. The remaining outcomes in table 10.3 show the impact of alternative marketing restrictions on Thompson's prescription sales efforts. The fourth outcome, creating the joint venture but allowing Thompson to actively market betaMANNx for two more years, maximizes the joint benefit available at $35.5 million.

While the joint venture loses $4 million ($30 million less $26 million) when Thompson markets betaMANNx for two years,

Thompson gains $6.5 million ($9.5 million less $3 million). This is a net increase of $2.5 million over the outcome if Thompson doesn't market the drug. While you may not like the active marketing, Thompson is likely to accept a smaller share of the joint venture's profit in order to keep marketing betaMANNx.

We combine the distributive and integrative analysis of the MANNx-OTC joint venture in figure 10.1, which plots Thompson's profit on the vertical axis and NN's profit on the horizontal axis. Line A is Thompson's $12 million reservation price, below which there will be no agreement. The various profit outcomes are represented by 45 degree lines to show the possible range of agreements after P is negotiated. For example, the points on the

Table 10.2 *Thompson's Payoff Table (in millions)*

Outcome	Lifetime Expected Profit to Thompson
No joint venture	$12
Joint venture: Thompson stops active marketing of betaMANNx immediately	$3+P
Joint venture: Thompson stops active marketing of betaMANNx after 1 year	$7+P
Joint venture: Thompson stops active marketing of betaMANNx after 2 years	$9.5+P
Joint venture: Thompson stops active marketing of betaMANNx after 3 years	$10.5+P
Joint venture: Thompson stops active marketing of betaMANNx after 4 years	$11+P
Joint venture: Thompson stops active marketing of betaMANNx after 5 years	$11.5+P
Joint venture: Thompson continues active marketing of betaMANNx throughout the product's remaining 6-year life	$12+P

most northeasterly line all yield profits of $35.5 million, while the points on other outcome lines lead to profits of between $30 million and $35 million.

An agreement on the most northeasterly line is in each company's best interest. It's better for Thompson to be as close to your reservation price as possible on this line, and it's better for you to be as close as possible to Thompson's. Both you and Thompson

Table 10.3 *Joint Profit—Sample Resolutions (in millions)*

Outcome	NN	T	NN + T	Synergy
No joint venture	$0	$12	$12	—
Joint venture: Thompson stops active marketing of betaMANNx immediately	$30-P	$3+P	$33	$21
Joint venture: Thompson stops active marketing of betaMANNx after 1 year	$28-P	$7+P	$35	$23
Joint venture: Thompson stops active marketing of betaMANNx after 2 years	$26-P	$9.5+P	$35.5	$23.5
Joint venture: Thompson stops active marketing of betaMANNx after 3 years	$24-P	$10.5+P	$34.5	$22.5
Joint venture: Thompson stops active marketing of betaMANNx after 4 years	$22-P	$11+P	$33	$21
Joint venture: Thompson stops active marketing of betaMANNx after 5 years	$20-P	$11.5+P	$31.5	$19.5
Joint venture: Thompson continues active marketing of betaMANNx throughout the product's remaining 6-year life	$18-P	$12+P	$30	$18

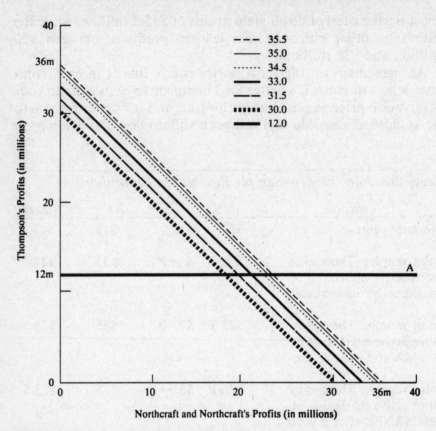

Figure 10.1 Combine Analysis of the MANNx-OTC Joint Venture

want to reach an integrative agreement and do as well as possible on the distributive issue, the transfer price. However, managers usually make the mistake of focusing on one dimension or the other, rather than on both dimensions simultaneously.

If you could get Thompson to agree to take only one-third of the profit for the joint venture in exchange for continuing to market betaMANNx, Thompson would receive $3 million plus one-third of $30 million for a total of $13 million, and you would receive two-thirds of $30 million or $20 million. While this is a fine agreement for you, Thompson could also have accepted an agreement that allowed two years of marketing (worth $9.5 million to them) and $4 million (of the $26 million available from the joint venture)—a better agreement for both sides. Thompson now gets $13.5 million instead of $13 million and you get $22 million instead of $20 million.

The northeasterly line represents the set of fully integrative agreements, since from any point on the line, you can't find any other agreement that would make both parties better off. However, once you've identified the fully integrative agreements, you still need to consider the distributive issue of how to share the additional joint benefit.

In figure 10.1, you see the central themes of thinking rationally in negotiation. Rational thinking must not be limited to only the distributive dimension or the integrative dimension. By organizing all available information, you can make more rational choices and increase your chances of reaching a fully integrative agreement that is also the best distributive agreement.

AUDITING FOR BIASES

Prescription 8: Assess the degree to which you might be affected by (a) the tendency to irrationally escalate commitment to a previously chosen strategy, (b) the mythical fixed-pie, (c) anchoring and adjustment, (d) the framing of the negotiation, (e) the availability of information, (f) the winner's curse, and (g) overconfidence.

One limitation of the rational thought process we've outlined is that it assumes you will use objective information in your analysis. Yet, we've also described how your information processing is biased. Fortunately, being mindful of the likely biases lets you actively evaluate how they can affect your decision making.

In representing NN, are you arguing for Thompson to stop all active marketing simply because that was your initial position? Or are you actively searching for trade-offs between marketing and profit sharing? Are you paying too much attention to Thompson's initial offer of $50 million and six years of marketing and allowing it to anchor your evaluation of what is possible? Are you looking at the problem from a limited frame, focusing on the joint venture rather than the combined interests of the two sides? Are you preoccupied by a vivid issue or concern such as getting at least 50 percent of the profit, and jeopardizing the value inherent in the joint venture itself? Are you thinking carefully about the other party's decision processes? Have you considered what Thompson may know about betaMANNx that you don't? Is there some objective way to check your assessment that your negotiation strategy will work? You must ask *and answer* these questions to avoid negotiating irrationally.

Prescription 9: Assess the degree to which your negotiation opponent might be affected by (a) the tendency to irrationally escalate commitment to a previously selected negotiation strategy, (b) the mythical fixed-pie, (c) anchoring and adjustment, (d) the framing of the negotiation, (e) the availability of information, (f) the winner's curse, and (g) overconfidence.

If the other side is making irrational decisions, it's hard to reach a rational agreement. If you can anticipate such biases, you can stop them from destroying the negotiation. For instance, you can help prevent Thompson from taking a public position that they will feel obligated to hold. You can help them see the mutual benefit of trade-offs. You can be careful to reject completely any unacceptable offer or anchor they propose. A common mistake is to acknowledge and respond to an unreasonable initial offer. Instead, you can reframe the negotiation by focusing your arguments on what Thompson has to gain from reaching an agreement with NN. Point out the information they might be valuing too much. Help Thompson see the negotiation from your perspective. Providing Thompson with more accurate information will reduce any overconfidence in their position. Finally, take Thompson's biases into account when formulating your own negotiation strategy.

It's essential to exchange information during negotiation. Often executives anchor on their initial understanding without taking advantage of the additional information that can emerge over the course of the negotiation. If you are too committed to persuading your opponent to concede, you will miss the important information you can glean from their verbal, and nonverbal, responses. Thus, you need to constantly update your information base, think about the other side's decisions, and formulate your negotiation strategy dynamically.

CHAPTER

11

Rational Strategies for Creating Integrative Agreements

In the last chapter, we gave you the information you needed about the other party's preferences to create mutually beneficial trade-offs. Remember, such information is usually something you have to work hard to discover. In this chapter, we identify twelve strategies to help you find the information you need to identify and evaluate these trade-offs. These strategies include how to collect information, how to cope with different perceptions among parties, how to use different perceptions to the advantage of both sides, and how to go beyond simple trade-offs to create truly integrative agreements.

No one strategy is perfect for all situations. We hope to provide a diverse set of approaches. You must decide which ones are appropriate for a particular situation. The effectiveness of the strategies varies with the level of trust between parties. In addition, it's possible to use one strategy early in the negotiation, and later switch to another strategy if the first one isn't helping you get all the information you need.

STRATEGIES FOR FINDING TRADE-OFFS

We focus in this section on five strategies for finding out the preferences of the other party in order to create favorable trade-offs.

BUILD TRUST AND SHARE INFORMATION

The easiest way to find the best integrative agreement in the MANNx-OTC case would be for both parties to share all their information. Then simple arithmetic is all that's needed to determine the outcome that maximizes joint benefit. Unfortunately, this is easier said than done. Executives in a negotiation often don't trust the other side and believe that such a strategy may give away critical information (such as reservation prices) that could reduce their advantage in the distributive dimension of the negotiation. Yet, if the goal is maximizing combined interests, sharing information is an ideal way for the two organizations to approach the task. It guarantees that there will be no dollars "left on the table" as the parties argue over how to divide the resource pie. The benefit from the extra joint profitability often outweighs the distributive gain that one side might get using more competitive tactics. In addition, sharing information helps create the positive relationship between the parties that is necessary for an ongoing joint venture. In joint ventures or any intra-organizational negotiations, information sharing should be a central strategy.

Sometimes parties may discuss a distribution rule before sharing information. For example, Thompson may fear they will be at a competitive disadvantage if NN knows they can only earn $12 million on their own. One strategy is to set a rule for sharing any surplus benefit, beyond what Thompson could earn on their own, before exchanging confidential information. For example, they might agree that NN gets 60 percent of the surplus. With this distributive understanding, they can then share information to create the best agreement. If the two sides distrust each other, they could also agree to an independent review of all the financial assessments.

Strategy 1: Build trust and share information.

ASK LOTS OF QUESTIONS

In certain circumstances, full information sharing won't be to your advantage. One side is often unwilling to agree to complete disclosure of confidential information—often with good reason. There may be information that *will* work against one side if the other party obtains it. The simple strategy of asking lots of questions can give you a significant amount of information—even if your opponent doesn't answer them all.

Most people tend to see negotiating as an opportunity to influence the other party. As a result, they talk more than they should and, instead of listening when the other side talks, they concentrate on what they're going to say next. To negotiate effectively, a manager needs to understand the other party's interests. Ask questions to find the information you need to create trade-offs: "How much would Thompson lose if they stopped their active marketing immediately?" "How much profit would be added if Thompson continued their marketing for two years?" The answers provide the basis for understanding the structure of Thompson's interests. While you may not get answers to all of your questions, you'll know more than if you hadn't asked any. In addition, you can learn from what isn't said as well as from what is.

Strategy 2: Ask lots of questions.

GIVE AWAY SOME INFORMATION

If trust between the parties is low, if your opponent is not answering questions in any useful way, giving away some information may break the informational deadlock. While an executive might not wish to specify his or her BATNA or reservation price, he or she can offer information concerning the relative importance of the issues to his or her side. For example, NN might volunteer that Thompson's actively marketing betaMANNx will cost the joint venture $2 million per year. NN hasn't revealed any information that Thompson can use distributively. However, this is useful information for Thompson and may help the two sides identify and implement trade-offs.

Behaviors in negotiation are often reciprocated.[1] When you scream at people, they tend to scream back. When you apologize to a negotiation opponent, they tend to apologize too. Likewise, when you give them some information, they tend to return some information. Just by providing some knowledge, you can stimulate the information sharing you need to create mutually beneficial agreements.

Strategy 3: Give away some information.

MAKE MULTIPLE OFFERS SIMULTANEOUSLY

Many managers want to state their position early in a negotiation to anchor the subsequent discussion. Unfortunately, this often happens before the relative interests and preference structure of the opponent are known. It's better to collect information before putting an offer on the table or responding to one. Yet many managers will feel compelled to respond before they have the information they need. Typically, they make a single offer. What if NN has offered Thompson $14 million—provided Thompson stops their active marketing immediately—and Thompson had rejected it? NN has learned very little. The negotiators for NN don't know why the offer was rejected, and they have learned nothing about the importance of the issues to Thompson.

Suppose NN had offered Thompson the following options: (a) $14 million of the profit from the joint venture if Thompson stops active marketing of betaMANNx immediately or (b) $12 million of the profit if Thompson stops marketing after one year or (c) $10 million of the profit if Thompson stops marketing after two years or (d) $8 million of the profit if Thompson stops active marketing of betaMANNx after three years or (e) $2 million of the profit if Thompson continues marketing betaMANNx for the remaining six years of the patent.

Thompson still rejects the offers, but NN can now ask which offer is closest to being acceptable. Thompson evaluates the proposals according to table 10.2, and sees that the proposals provide a net profit of $17 million, $19 million, $19.5 million,

$18.5 million, and $14 million respectively. Thompson can now respond with some confidence that of these unacceptable proposals, "c" is most reasonable. NN now has information to help them form a fully integrative agreement. All five proposals were equally valuable to NN and they revealed no more information by posing the range of alternatives than would be disclosed by making only one offer. Yet, by making multiple offers simultaneously, NN collects valuable information *and* appears more flexible.

Strategy 4: Make multiple offers simultaneously.

SEARCH FOR POST-SETTLEMENT SETTLEMENTS

We must recognize that a lot of disputes are settled by hardnosed, positional bargaining. Settled, yes. But efficiently settled? Often not. . . . They quibble about sharing the pie and often fail to realize that perhaps the pie can be jointly enlarged. . . . There may be another carefully crafted settlement that both (parties) might prefer to the settlement they actually achieved.[2]

By devising the concept of the post-settlement settlement (PSS), Howard Raiffa has developed a promising new approach to minimizing irrational negotiation. His basic idea is that managers who reach a mutually acceptable agreement can ask a third party to help them find a more fully integrative agreement. During the PSS process, each side reserves the right to veto the PSS proposed by the third party and retain the original agreement.

We argue that executives should look for a PSS, without the help of a third party, as a last step to assure they reach an integrative agreement.[3] After an initial agreement is reached, you can propose to look for a better one for both sides, but agree to be bound by the initial agreement if another isn't found. However, if you do find a better agreement, then you both share the surplus.

If NN and Thompson reached agreement on a joint venture that provided Thompson with $12 million, providing they stop all active marketing immediately, their profit would be $15 million and NN's profit would be $18 million. With a PSS process, they could better share information to create an agreement worth $1.25 million more to both sides by revising their agreement to include payment of $6.75 million to Thompson and freedom to actively market betaMANNx for two years. This PSS would provide Thompson with a profit of $16.25 million and NN a profit of $19.25 million. Clearly, this PSS is to the advantage of both parties. A PSS process offers a final chance for the parties to find a fully efficient agreement with limited risk to either party.

Strategy 5: Search for post-settlement settlements.

These five strategies offer you a variety of ideas for constructing fully integrative agreements. You need to remember, however, that an integrative strategy rarely eliminates the distributive aspect of negotiation; in fact, any integrative advice is incomplete if it fails to consider the distributive dimension. By having frameworks for thinking about both dimensions, you can improve overall performance for everyone involved.

USING DIFFERENCES TO CREATE INTEGRATIVE AGREEMENTS

Many negotiations break down because the parties can't resolve their differences. But you need to learn to think of differences as opportunities rather than barriers.[4] We discuss three such differences: assessments of the probability of future events (expectations), risk preferences, and time preferences.

DIFFERENCES IN EXPECTATIONS

In the MANNx-OTC negotiations, NN had a set of assessments about the profitability of the joint venture (table 10.1). Assume that Thompson also had their own assessments. Suppose Thompson projected that the joint venture would earn $80 million with no active marketing, $78 million with one year of marketing, and so forth. This would create an initial barrier to agreement; different assessments of the size of the pie will lead to differing estimates of the magnitude of each share. While Thompson might expect their portion of the profit to be around $40 million, NN would never pay that amount regardless of which agreement is selected. Without trust between the two, NN would have a hard time convincing Thompson of the accuracy of their $30 million forecast. Impasse would seem inevitable.

Now consider the following agreement: Thompson stops active marketing of betaMANNx after two years, NN gets the first $20 million of profit, and Thompson gets 80 percent of any profit over $20 million. This allows each party to bet on their belief about the future. If either company's forecast is correct, this agreement is much better for them than receiving 50 percent of the overall profit of the joint venture. While they won't both be right, basing their trade on differing expectations increases their chances of reaching agreement. This type of arrangement, known as a *contingent contract,* takes advantage of different beliefs, creating an opportunity for trade in which both parties believe they will do well because of the uncertainty of their forecasts.

Mark Twain noted that "it is difference of opinion that makes horse races."[5] Contingent contracts are bets that allow the parties to agree, even when they have different perceptions or opinions of the future. Rather than discussing how NN and Thompson share the profit, the negotiation is about their sharing the profit if X occurs, if Y occurs, if Z occurs, etc. The two sides' different expectations about these issues, similar to their different preferences on multiple issues, enhances the flexibility of the negotiation, increasing the chances for a trade.

Strategy 6: Use differences of expectations to create mutually beneficial perceived trade-offs.

DIFFERENCES IN RISK PREFERENCES

NN and Thompson might agree on their forecast of the expected profit of the joint venture, but also agree that they are only estimates. While they might agree that with Thompson actively marketing betaMANNx, the joint venture is expected to earn $26 million, they might think the actual amount could be anywhere between $10 million and $42 million. Now assume that Thompson is very concerned that they receive at least $8 million from the joint venture in order to make it acceptable to the skeptics in their organization who think Thompson should stay out of the risky over-the-counter marketplace. NN, on the other hand, is willing to take risks if they are rewarded for it. Therefore, Thompson is comparatively more risk-averse than NN. Thompson might reject an offer that split the profit of the joint venture equally, since the lowest end of their expectations projects a profit below $8 million.

Different risk preferences increase the number of possible alternatives in a dispute. A possible trade-off would be to offer Thompson more guaranteed money and NN more of the potential return. Perhaps Thompson could continue to market betaMANNx for two years, receive a payment of $8 million from NN, and 10 percent of the profit above the $8 million. Thompson gets its guarantee, and NN gets a higher expected return for taking the higher risk.

Rather than seeing one party's relative risk aversion as an obstacle to negotiation, you can use it as an opportunity to trade. One side gets a guarantee in return for increasing the expected value to the other. Different risk-sharing strategies allow for trades that might not otherwise occur.

Strategy 7: Use differences of risk preferences to create mutually beneficial perceived trade-offs.

DIFFERENCES IN TIME PREFERENCES

Assume that Thompson is having a year so poor' that it affects their priorities in the negotiation. They need immediate profitability in the early years of the joint venture. NN, however, is more concerned with the overall profitability. Assuming the product will be equally profitable over its six-year life, it might not be as attractive to Thompson to split the profit as it is earned. Both sides might be happier with an agreement in which Thompson gets 80 percent of the profits, and NN gets 20 percent, from the first three years and Thompson gets 10 percent, and NN gets 90 percent, of the profit from years four through six. Thompson is assured of receiving their desired return immediately, and NN is rewarded with higher future profits for delaying their return. The parties have again found an issue on which to base a trade, their different time preferences for receiving profit.

Often, when an opponent is adamant about some issue (like

receiving earlier payment), it's a signal that there's an opportunity for a trade. When time preference differences exist, you can often rearrange future payoffs to give earlier return to the more impatient party. Whether they are due to individual differences, cultural differences, or the specific situations of the parties, these differences should be seen as opportunities for, not as barriers to agreement.

Strategy 8: Use different time preferences to create mutually beneficial trade-offs.

ADDITIONAL STRATEGIES FOR CREATING INTEGRATIVE AGREEMENTS

The first eight strategies for finding integrative agreements involve finding trade-offs across issues, the most common way to create joint gain. Dean Pruitt has identified four additional strategies that move beyond finding trade-offs.[6] Consider the following:

ABC Inc., a consumer-oriented manufacturer, has identified an outstanding recruit from a high-caliber competitor whom both the marketing and sales departments would like to hire. Each department wants to use this woman's skills as a systems analyst, and values her background in consumer goods. Like many organizations, ABC is rapidly computerizing their internal systems. However, the number of people trained in both the nature of the industry and computer systems is limited. The immediate problem is how to deal internally with the two departments who want to hire this recruit. How should they resolve the conflict?

A couple of obvious solutions exist. The two departments could use a free-market approach and compete against each other to hire the recruit. However, ABC is likely to end up paying more than necessary to hire her, and the process will probably seem peculiar to the recruit. Another obvious alternative is to compromise, for example, by splitting her time, 50 percent in marketing and 50 percent in sales. This leads to a number of administrative problems, however, and at least one of the departments is likely to feel that 50 percent of the time isn't enough.

Both of these solutions *assume* that the two departments must split a fixed resource, namely the recruit. In contrast an integrative solution, trading-off issues, can be found in the two computerization issues facing both departments: (1) the long-term need to hire qualified computer professionals and (2) the immediate need to handle the work of merging the sales and marketing databases. While it's obvious the recruit would be valuable to either department, the primary interests of the two may be different. Marketing may be more concerned with the first issue while sales may be more interested in the second. Thus, an agreement in which the marketing department hires the recruit, but assigns her full responsibility for the database merger, trades-off the two issues.

Managers should identify a number of alternative integrative strategies, since your primary strategy may run into resistance in the negotiation. Pruitt's work moves beyond trade-off strategies to suggest that managers can reach integrative outcomes by adding issues to the table. Some techniques include making it less costly for your opponent to compromise on the primary issue, adding more resources to the negotiation, and finding a solution that doesn't exactly meet either side's stated position, but addresses their underlying interests. While they're similar to finding trade-offs, these strategies focus on added ways to find mutually beneficial agreements.

ADDING ISSUES TO THE NEGOTIATION

By adding issues to a negotiation, one party might get what they want in the original negotiation, while compensating the other party on some additional, unrelated issue. For example, assume that the sales and marketing departments also were arguing about which department should pay for the new database. The sales department could agree to hire the recruit and also pay for the mutually desired database. By adding issues to the negotiation, you can move away from a distributive perspective and increase your potential for a trade-off.

Strategy 9: Consider adding issues to the negotiation to increase the potential for making mutually beneficial trade-offs.

COST-CUTTING

The cost-cutting strategy calls for one party to get what it wants while the other has the costs associated with its concession reduced or eliminated. The result is a high level of joint benefit, not because one party "wins," but because the other party suffers less. What if the recruit is both highly priced and highly skilled and, while the marketing department values all her skills, the sales department simply needs someone with computer skills. In an integrative agreement, marketing could hire the recruit and transfer a less skilled employee (with a lower salary) to the sales department.

Cost-cutting means the party who makes the major concession receives something to meet the specific goals they gave up. While similar to a trade-off, this is a unique strategy that emphasizes **reducing** or eliminating the costs to one side of letting the other **side** achieve its objectives.

Strategy 10: Consider whether there is some way to reduce the costs to the other party of allowing you to get what you want, and vice versa.

OBTAINING ADDED RESOURCES

The recruiting problem, as with many conflicts, is largely due to a resource shortage. There aren't enough skilled recruits to meet the current needs of the organization. Another integrative option is to expand the available resources. Can another recruit be found? If so, each department can get what it wants.

Obtaining added resources is a useful strategy when such resources exist, but it's only viable when the parties' interests are not mutually exclusive. The marketing department's interest in hiring a consumer-oriented systems analyst can't conflict with the sales department's interests. However, there are many conflicts in which the parties' interests are mutually exclusive and obtaining added resources is unlikely to be a successful integrative strategy.

Strategy 11: Consider whether there is some way to reduce or eliminate the scarcity of the resource that is creating the conflict between the two parties.

SEARCHING FOR A NOVEL SOLUTION NOT CURRENTLY UNDER DISCUSSION

This strategy calls for creating a new solution focusing on both parties' underlying interests. While neither side achieves its initial objective, creative options are found by redefining the conflict. For example, assume that both sales and marketing want the following benefits from hiring the recruit: (1) the employee's skills; (2) the ability to use these skills over an extended period of time; and (3) the department's share of the work done on the database merger. You can bridge these desires by hiring the recruit into a staff position in the Management Information Systems Department, with the understanding that she would initially work on the sales/marketing database merger, and be available for special future projects in both departments.

This is a reformulation of the conflict that demands a clear understanding of each party's underlying interests. Creative solutions can be found by redefining the conflict for each side, identifying their underlying interests, and brainstorming for a wide variety of potential solutions.

Strategy 12: Search for novel solutions to the negotiation that do not meet either party's stated position, but do meet their underlying interests.

These last four strategies for identifying integrative agreements require that at least one party move beyond the existing definition of the conflict. Finding creative solutions that lie outside the assumptions of the conflict is a useful way to increase the joint resources each side can share.

CONCLUSIONS

We've now completed our prescriptive advice for identifying rational negotiation solutions. While you have to use the strategies selectively, having them all available reduces your chances of reaching inefficient solutions. In the third section of the book, we build upon the concepts and prescriptions we've presented as we increase the complexity of the negotiations.

THREE

Simplifying Complex Negotiations

CHAPTER

12

Are You an Expert?

Many of you probably have lots of negotiation experience. Does having a lot of experience make you an expert? If not, what does true expertise require? In this chapter, we answer this question by examining the distinction between experience and expertise in negotiation. We also consider how you can best combine your experience with our framework for thinking rationally to improve the overall effectiveness of your negotiating skills.

Expertise, to many people, means the ability to get good results. This definition really doesn't explain the true nature of expertise. Many people are experts, yet they don't always get good outcomes. How can this be explained?

Focusing only on results ignores a critical factor in an expert's ability to produce good outcomes—the role of uncertainty. While you'd like to be able to rely on experts to make decisions that always result in good outcomes, experts, like everyone, often make their choices in the face of uncertainty. Thus, experts can make decisions that have poor results, and novices can make decisions that have great results.

Think about how you might decide what wine to buy. In choosing among the different kinds, you may rely on experts' reviews. The recent reviews of Chateau Potelle's 1988 chardonnay illustrate how easily it is for acknowledged experts to disagree. The chardonnay got great reviews from *The Wine Spectator,* which reported, "Smooth, concentrated and well-behaved . . . deep fruit flavors and a sense of intensity . . . delicious to drink now but it could be cellared until 1992." It was given a rating of 88 out of 100 points. But the review in *The Wine Advocate* read, "Here is another bitterly acidic, austere, lean, thin wine . . . no pleasure, no character and no soul." The same wine got 67 out of 100 points. Both of these experts can't be right. So, if you were looking for a good white wine, would you consider Chateau Potelle's 1988 chardonnay?[1]

While these two publications are marketed as offering expert opinions, the differences could just be chalked up to differences in the reviewers' personal tastes. Experts also often disagree on what should be purely factual information, such as how to prepare the taxes for a family of four. Each March, *Money* magazine publishes the results of the following "test."

> During each of the last four years, fifty professional tax preparers were asked to complete a 1040 form for a hypothetical family of four. In 1988, no two preparers computed the same amount of tax due—their figures ranged from $7,202 to $11,881. In 1989, the preparers reported taxes due ranging from $12,539 to $35,831. In the 1990 test, the hypothetical family had an annual income of $132,000 and the taxes due ranged from $9,806 to $21,216. In the 1991 test, only one preparer reported to *Money* the correct tax of $16,786 on an annual income of just under $200,000. The other 48 returns (one preparer did not submit a return) reported taxes due ranging from $6,807 to $73,247 and, as in the past four years, there were almost as many different answers as there were tax preparers. In addition, each year *Money* found no connection between the fees the preparers charged their clients and performance. In 1991, the best performing preparer, and the two worst, all charged around the same, average fee of $86 per hour.[2]

If experts cannot agree, then what about novices? You can probably think of people you know who've gotten great deals, not because of any specific expertise, but just because they happened to be in the right place at the right time. Consider the deal a twelve-year-old baseball card collector got.

> Twelve-year-old Brian Wrzensinski bought a Nolan Ryan "rookie" card for $12 from a baseball-card store in Addison, Illinois. It turns out that the card is worth somewhere between $800 and $1200.[3] Brian bought the card a few days after the store had opened for business. It was quite busy and

the owner had asked a clerk from a nearby jewelry store to help out. The substitute clerk didn't know anything about baseball or baseball cards. When Brian asked if the card cost $12, the clerk looked at the $1200 price and interpreted it as $12—the price she charged Brian. While Brian didn't know exactly how much the card was worth, he did say that he had seen similar cards for $150 and up. "I knew the card was worth more than $12," he said. "I just offered $12 for it and the lady sold it to me. People go into card shops and try to bargain all the time."[4]

"Even a blind hog picks up an acorn every now and again."

Great outcomes can happen—a blind hog can occasionally find acorns or a twelve-year-old baseball card collector can buy an extremely rare card for $12—but not because of true expertise. Such lucky outcomes cannot be predicted or relied on.

Thus, experts err and novices succeed—sometimes. Complete success in negotiation is not a reasonable goal. Your goal should be to develop the ability to make better negotiated decisions most of the time. The true test of an expert is: over the course of multiple negotiations, are they better able to get good results?

EXPERIENCE VERSUS EXPERTISE

Luck aside, a manager can get high-quality negotiation outcomes in two ways: (1) he or she may learn an effective pattern of behavior for a particular situation, without necessarily being able to generalize this knowledge to related situations, or (2) negotiate rationally by selecting strategies that are appropriate to the goals, opponents, and other factors that are unique to the situation. While it can be hard to distinguish these two processes in a particular negotiation, the differences become obvious when the situation changes. To get high-quality results across situations and over time, and thus move closer to expertise, you must combine your experience with the rational negotiation prescriptions we've defined.

Experience is very useful. It helps you understand which factors are important in a particular negotiation. Unfortunately, experience alone doesn't guarantee good outcomes because it's typically limited to the situations in which it was developed. While you may be the top sales person in your organization because of your consummate skill at closing negotiations, this doesn't mean you can negotiate with your spouse successfully. The strategies you use at work won't be as successful in this other, very different form of negotiation.

Robyn Dawes, a psychologist, highlights the drawbacks of learning only from experience.[5] He notes that Benjamin Franklin's famous quote "experience is a dear teacher" is often misinterpreted to mean "experience is the best teacher." Dawes asserts what Franklin really meant was "experience is an expensive teacher," because Franklin goes on to observe "yet fools will learn in no other [school]." Dawes writes,

> Learning from an experience of failure . . . is indeed "dear," and it can even be fatal. . . . Moreover, experiences of success may have negative as well as positive results when people mindlessly learn from them . . . people who are extraordinarily successful—or lucky—in general may conclude from their "experience" that they are invulnerable and consequently court disaster by failing to monitor their behavior and its implications.

Consider the recent history of labor/management relations in the United States. In the 1960s, both sides had some very experienced negotiators. When the United States became less economically competitive, labor and management continued to use old negotiation strategies in this new, more competitive environment. This led to a disastrous period of layoffs for organized labor and declines in U.S. manufacturing productivity. These negotiators had considerable experience, but they lacked the necessary expertise to adapt their strategies to the new global negotiating environment. While there clearly were other factors that led to the decline of American industry, the rigidity of labor-management relations certainly contributed.

Experience by itself, however, does not prepare you to adapt to new situations. Think about the simple task of getting a cab. You are in town for business and staying at a large hotel. How do you get a taxi? Probably, you just step outside, tell the doorman where you wish to go, and he'll hail a cab for you. No big deal.

Now suppose you weren't in New York or some other major U.S. city, but in Bangkok, Thailand, staying at the prestigious Oriental Hotel. If you needed a cab, the doorman at the Oriental would hail one for you and tell the driver where you wished to go. The taxi would cost about what you would expect. However, if you had walked down the street about twenty feet and gotten your own cab, the price of the same ride would be about 75 percent lower. You would never know about this price discrimination if you simply followed your experience-based model of getting a taxi because, in the U.S., walking the extra twenty feet wouldn't save you money.

What you learn from experience is obviously limited by the experiences you've had. Thus, in negotiation, it's also true that your ability to adapt what you've experienced to other situations is also limited.

LEARNING FROM EXPERIENCE—WHY IS IT SO DIFFICULT?

Learning from experience is common enough. You are often in new situations and you learn how to behave through a process of trial and error. You act in a certain way and then monitor the results to figure out what to do or not to do in the future. Economists argue that this experience and feedback process can, for example, protect experts from the "winner's curse" problem we discussed in Chapter 7.

> Given sufficient experience and feedback regarding the outcomes of their decisions . . . most bidders in "real world" settings would eventually learn to avoid the winner's curse in any particular set of circumstances. The winner's curse is a disequilibrium phenomenon that will correct itself given sufficient time and the right kind of information feedback.[6]

However, to learn from experience you need accurate and immediate feedback, and this is often not available. As Amos Tversky and Danny Kahneman suggest:

> . . . (i) outcomes are commonly delayed and not easily attributable to a particular action; (ii) variability in the

environment degrades the reliability of feedback . . . ; (iii) there is often no information about what the outcome would have been if another decision had been taken; and (iv) most important decisions are unique and therefore provide little opportunity for learning . . . any claim that a particular error will be eliminated by experience must be supported by demonstrating that the conditions for effective learning are satisfied.[7]

It's often difficult for executives to determine what types of feedback they need to evaluate the accuracy of their decisions. Selecting one alternative or making one set of choices often precludes your knowing the outcomes of other alternatives or choices—except in situations such as horse races where, after a race, you know not only whether the horse you bet on won, but how all the other horses you could have bet on finished. It's hard to learn much from a chosen course of action if you can't compare your results to the unchosen, alternative outcomes.

Even with feedback about your performance, it's still difficult to learn from experience. In a recent study using the "Acquiring a Company" exercise we described earlier, we asked MBA students to respond to repeated presentations of the problem.[8] We wanted to test their ability to incorporate the decisions of "others" (a computer played the role of the target firm) into their own decision making. The study used real money, and participants played twenty times. The results from each decision were reported to them immediately, and they could see how their asset balance changed (virtually always downward).

Remembering that $0 is the correct answer and that $50 to $75 is the typical answer, look at the mean bids across the twenty trials in figure 12.1. There is no obvious improvement—the average response hovers between $50 and $60. In fact, only five of sixty-nine participants ever discovered the correct solution (bidding $0) over the twenty trials. Thus, experience, even when coupled with feedback, failed to help participants improve their performance.

OVERCOMING BARRIERS TO LEARNING FROM EXPERIENCE

The major barrier to learning effectively from experience is, as we've suggested, that feedback about successful strategies is often

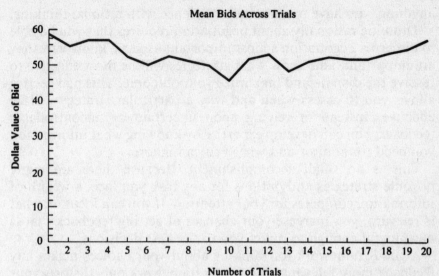

Figure 12.1   "Acquiring a Company"—The Lack of Learning

unclear, delayed, or not given in a meaningful way. In addition, executives often have a psychological investment in the choices they make, reducing how open they are to feedback about their decisions. If a manager's self-esteem depends on the outcome of the decision, this can make him or her see ambiguous feedback as more positive than it really is.[9]

Consider how difficult it is for your employees to hear and incorporate negative performance evaluations. Faculty often seem unable to hear (or let themselves acknowledge) negative feedback in their contract renewal or tenure review process. Most faculty who are denied tenure say they are surprised by the decision, regardless of the amount and type of negative feedback previously conveyed to them and documented in their personnel records.

Even if managers correctly understand relevant and meaningful feedback, that information still must be stored in their memory and then retrieved to be considered in later decisions. As we discussed earlier, memory storage and retrieval are influenced by many irrelevant factors. We are not contesting that people learn from experience—that is obviously true. We believe, however, that learning from experience does not usually produce the type of understanding that you need for true expertise. To be an expert at anything, you have to combine experience with rational thinking.

Thinking rationally about negotiation requires that you be able to discern a negotiation's most important aspects, know why they are important, and know what strategies will be most effective to resolve the dispute and maximize your outcome. This perspective allows you to assess when and why a particular strategy will be effective. Instead of relying upon uncertain or uncontrollable feedback, you can develop expertise by knowing what information you need to monitor and what you can ignore.

This is no small accomplishment. Because there are many possible strategies and options for any task you face, a wealth of information competes for your attention. If you can focus on what is relevant, you increase your chances of getting feedback that is meaningful enough to direct you to the best decisions.

A good framework for thinking about your choices makes any feedback more relevant. The wrong framework only distorts your perceptions and your judgment.

Consider a study in which we examined the ability of negotiators to generalize their experience in one situation to other, similar situations.[10] Negotiators participated in either a distributive or an integrative negotiation. The results were quite consistent: regardless of the type of negotiation first experienced, negotiators didn't do well when confronted with a *new* negotiation task that incorporated *both* distributive and integrative components. We then gave half of each of the groups training that matched their experience. Half of the subjects who had experienced a distributive negotiation received distributively oriented training; half of the subjects who experienced an integrative negotiation received integratively oriented training. The results were very interesting.

Those with both training and experience negotiated significantly better outcomes than those with experience alone. With training about the concepts behind negotiation, they were better able to think rationally about their own negotiation. Moreover, integratively trained negotiators outperformed distributively trained negotiators who outperformed negotiators with integrative experience but no training. We concluded that, for managers, integrative training will provide the greatest advantage.

What this suggests is that your experience by itself won't improve your outcomes, but having a conceptual framework of negotiation will. Further, we found a clear competitive advantage to integrative training that we didn't find with distributive training.

TURNING EXPERIENCE INTO EXPERTISE

Two main factors distinguish experience from expertise: (1) the ability of an expert to adapt his or her skills to get good outcomes, even in the face of new demands, and (2) the ability to transmit or transfer these skills, not only to new situations, but also to other people. By itself, experience often doesn't give you the skills to critically analyze the situations you find yourself in. To transform experience into expertise, you must understand what you've experienced, distinguish what makes successful experiences different from unsuccessful experiences, and develop a conceptual understanding of the process. Thus, if you can understand the factors that lead to success, you can adapt your experience to new situations and transfer your knowledge about what does and doesn't work to similar situations, and to other people.

Adaptability. Expertise is adaptable. While most experienced managers may be effective in very specific situations, when the context changes, their experience can actually become a hindrance. If negotiation expertise is the ability to adapt one's knowledge to a wide variety of negotiating situations, then this implies considerably more than experience. True experts should perform better and be able to adapt their strategies to each situation because they understand why particular strategies are effective. Expertise means having strategies that are sufficiently abstract or general to transfer across situations and settings.

By training the negotiators in our study, we were trying to give them a more complete conceptual understanding of negotiation. We found that this training allowed the negotiators to generalize the negotiation expertise developed in one situation (the original negotiation) to a second, unrelated situation.

Transferability. The second benefit of developing expertise instead of relying solely on experience is transferability. You've probably asked friends or colleagues who are particularly good at something how they do it. A common response is that it takes years of practice and patience to develop their level of skill. What this could really mean is that they can't explain what they do.

This reinforces the notion that their skill is an art, not a science. But if experienced managers can't articulate what makes them successful, they can't teach what they know to others—a critical part of being a good manager. Thus, a final drawback of experience alone is that it limits an executive's ability to transfer knowledge efficiently to future generations.

CONCLUSIONS

In this chapter, we've emphasized a primary way to improve your performance in a negotiation: the development of expertise by combining experience with the ability to think rationally. By understanding the demands of a particular problem and thinking rationally, you can improve your ability to analyze and restructure a proposed negotiation.

The question still remains, however, whether expertise in negotiation can lessen or eliminate the impact of the biases we've discussed on important, real-world decisions. The evidence suggests that expertise can clearly improve the quality of negotiated agreements and reduce the impact of some but not all biases.

In our study of expert negotiators facing a new situation, we found that they were susceptible to the framing bias, but did not fall prey to the mythical fixed-pie bias.[11] In our real estate agents study in Chapter 4, we found that the experts were able to outline a strategy for their appraisals that should have reduced the anchoring-and-adjustment bias, but didn't. The real estate agents failed to think rationally, perhaps because they couldn't get adequate feedback without access to objective market values to compare to their estimates. While the agents may have understood what they were supposed to do, they had little idea if they were, in fact, doing it.[12]

There are other factors, such as restructuring how information is used in making decisions, that may make thinking rationally about negotiation more effective in reducing bias. We found that simply changing the way information is presented can limit the impact of the anchoring-and-adjustment bias.

In another study, we examined the impact on managers of simultaneous versus sequential presentation of information on potential job candidates. We found that managers used the number of available positions (one or three) as anchors when they were presented twenty candidates simultaneously but not when the candidates were presented one at a time. When the candidates were presented simultaneously, significantly more of them were selected for interviews when there were three openings than when there was one. The number of openings made no difference when candidates were evaluated sequentially. But the managers did not realize this anchoring effect. When asked about the importance of number of openings in determining who and how many should be interviewed, they reported that it was relatively unimportant compared to such considerations as technical ability.[13]

A primary goal of this book is to develop your expertise as a negotiator. This requires a broad understanding of the important factors in negotiation. In the first two sections of the book, we laid the groundwork for thinking rationally about negotiation. In the subsequent chapters, we emphasize more advanced concepts of negotiation, beyond the simple two-person cases we've focused on thus far. In doing so, we begin to explore how the social context within which most negotiations occur can influence the thoughts, expectations, and (ultimately) the behavior of managers in a negotiation.

CHAPTER

13

Fairness, Emotion, and Rationality in Negotiation

Our focus on rational thinking may make you think that fairness and emotion should be ignored in negotiation. On the contrary, to negotiate successfully, managers must understand and anticipate the impact of emotional considerations and perceptions of fairness. The central purpose of this chapter is to integrate these concerns within our framework of negotiating rationally. Consider the following opportunity:

> You are walking down the street when you are approached by an eccentric-looking man who introduces himself to you and another pedestrian (Chris) whom you don't know. He holds up a thousand dollar bill and says, "I will give you this $1,000 bill providing that you can agree on how to split the money. In splitting up the money, however, there are two rules I will impose. First, Chris must decide how this $1,000 is to be split between the two of you and then you will decide whether or not to accept the split. If you do, then you and Chris will receive the $1,000 based on Chris's allocation. If you do not accept the split, then you each will receive nothing." Both you and Chris agree to play the game. Chris thinks for a moment and then says, "I propose that the $1000 be split as follows: I get $950 and you get $50." Now it is up to you; will you agree to this split?

If you're like most people, you will reject this split. Why? Rejecting such a deal isn't economically rational because you'd each be better off (+$950 for Chris and +$50 for you) if you accept.

However, there are many reasons why you might reject this offer—reasons that aren't found in the rational negotiation framework we've described so far. One such reason might be that you feel angry at Chris for placing you in this situation. But if you didn't think about fairness or your emotions, you would probably accept the $50. After all, $50 is better than nothing.

Now assume that the roles were reversed. You could decide the split and Chris could accept or reject it. What would you decide? If you didn't consider fairness or emotion, you could easily conclude that Chirs would accept the $50 (or less). But this proposal would probably leave you with $0—Chris would be likely to reject it. If you did think about fairness and emotion, however, you could better anticipate Chris' likely response, offer significantly more than $50, and improve your chances of making money on the deal. In this chapter, we focus on ways you can better understand your own concerns for fairness and your emotional reactions, and better anticipate the same concerns from your negotiation opponents.

FAIRNESS, RATIONALITY, AND NEGOTIATION

Fairness (or unfairness) is not an objective state. It's very difficult to predict what another person might consider a fair or unfair outcome. A fair outcome might be to allocate a negotiation's resources equally—each party gets the same amount of the benefit. Another fair distribution could be to reward the parties based on how much they've contributed. This is the basic notion behind incentives and merit-based compensation systems. A very different option is to distribute resources based on the parties' relative needs.[1] All these options might be considered fair because everybody has their own concepts about what's fair and will use them in making decisions.

Daniel Kahneman, Jack Knetsch and Richard Thaler demonstrated in a study that considerations of fairness often dominate purely economic considerations.[2] Suppose a hardware store sells snow shovels for $15. The morning after a large snowstorm, the store owner raises the price to $20. What is your opinion? Is this fair or unfair?

From an economic perspective, the price should go up. When

demand increases relative to supply, a price increase is expected. Despite this economic rationale, 82 percent of the respondents in the study considered raising the price of the snow shovels unfair. And, of those who said it was fair, many did not think it would be fair for a hardware store to raise the price of generators after a hurricane—even though the logic is basically the same.

Now reverse the situation and assume that you are the hardware store owner. You have twenty-five shovels left. Should you raise the price by $5? Even if you believe that the market is a fair measure of the shovels' value, you might say "no." But if you ignore concerns of fairness, you could raise the price and collect an additional $125 on the shovels. However, making that extra $125 now could cost you more in future business. While you may think your customers should understand the nature of the supply/demand relationship, if they think the price increase is unfair, they may stop coming to your store. Thus, if you act in an economically rational manner (e.g., increase the price of the shovels), you may lose out to competitors who take fairness into account, since your customers may take their business elsewhere.

The same biases that affect negotiation also influence perceptions of fairness. The Kahneman, Knetsch, and Thaler study demonstrated that judgments of fairness can be susceptible to the effects of framing. The following two problems were presented to the participants in the study:

Question A: A company is making a small profit. It is located in a community experiencing a recession with substantial unemployment but no inflation. There are many workers anxious to work at the company. The company decides to decrease wages and salaries 7 percent this year.

Sixty-two percent of the respondents thought the company's behavior was unfair.

Question B: A company is making a small profit. It is located in a community experiencing a recession with substantial unemployment and an inflation rate of 12 percent. There are many workers anxious to work at the company. The company decides to increase wages and salaries 5 percent this year.

In this case, only twenty-two percent of the participants thought the company's behavior was unfair. Despite the similar changes in real income, the way the problem was framed affected how fairness was judged. A wage cut was considered unfair, while a nominal gain that would not even cover inflation was more acceptable.

People seem to have their own "rules" of fair behavior. For example, they think wages should go up, not down. Thus, it's very difficult for employees to see a pay cut as fair, even when economic conditions change for the worse for a company. People think of money as an arbitrary unit (a dollar) rather than in terms of its real buying power (real dollars), which changes with inflation. Assessments of fairness in this area largely depend on whether wages follow these social rules.

At the beginning of the chapter, we described an example of "ultimatum bargaining."[3] In this type of game, two players (who typically do not know each other) are randomly assigned to be either Player 1 or Player 2. Player 1 is given a sum of money, say $10, that must be divided between the players. Player 1 must propose an allocation, and Player 2 must either accept or reject it. If Player 2 accepts, then the $10 is divided accordingly. If Player 2 rejects the proposed allocation, then neither player gets any money.

If all that counted in this game was the money, then Player 1 should allocate the smallest possible amount, say $.01, to Player 2. Player 2 should accept it because he or she will be better off gaining a penny than by refusing the allocation and gaining nothing. We've seen groups play this game, with very interesting results. Those acting as Player 1 almost never proposed a $9.99/$.01 division of the money. Very few Player 1's were even willing to propose a $9/$1 split. In fact, a fifty-fifty split was the most common allocation. If Player 1 tried to get an excessive amount of money, Player 2 typically refused to accept, leaving both players with nothing. From an economic standpoint, a Player 2 who turned down any amount of money was acting irrationally. However, we've described how this irrationality can be expected and explained. From a rational perspective, Player 1 should realize that Player 2 will be influenced by fairness considerations and offer significantly more than $.01.

In a variation of this called the Dictator Game, Player 1 can unilaterally decide how to allocate the $10 and Player 2 must accept the decision. Only thirty-six percent of Player 1's took all the money.[4] Although when acceptance by Player 2 was required, the proposals were more equal, sixty-four percent of Player 1's in the Dictator Game still chose to give the other party *some* money. Thus, people don't necessarily follow a rational economic model when they consider both fairness and the potential costs of unfairness.

There is a lot of evidence to suggest people prefer equal over unequal outcomes, regardless of the reason or situation. Another common influence on judgments of fairness is social comparison —comparing what one person gets to what others receive. One example of the effect of social comparison is illustrated by passages from "The Russian Character," *New York Times Magazine*, October 28, 1990 (pp. 31–71) by Hedrick Smith, the former Moscow bureau chief for the *New York Times* (copyright ©1990 by The New York Times Company; reprinted by permission):

> Russians are long-suffering people who can bear misery, so long as they see others are sharing it. But let someone become better off—even if it is through his own honest labor—and the collective jealousy can be fierce.
>
> I came to see the great mass of Soviet people as protagonists in what I call the culture of envy—corrosive animosity that took root under the czars in the deep seated collectivism in Russian life and then was accentuated by Leninist ideology.
>
> What is ominous for Gorbachev's reforms is that this free-floating anger of the rank and file often settles on anyone who rises above the crowd. This hostility is a serious danger to the new entrepreneurs Gorbachev is trying to nurture.
>
> I heard of a farmer outside Moscow whose horse and few cows were set free and whose barn was set afire by neighboring farm workers jealous of his modest prosperity.

The importance of equality as a criterion in judging fairness should not be underestimated, even in situations where some may wish to maintain equality simply to make sure that things are equally bad for everybody. Those who might end up with less through another distribution rule are usually the ones who want to use equality as the basis for sharing in the good and the bad.

That many people prefer equality as the basis for allocating both good and bad probably accounts, in large measure, for the prevalence of compromise in negotiation. That is, you and I begin a negotiation with some set of offers; the final solution is often achieved by splitting the difference between our initial positions or between the last two offers made. For example, consider how you might settle on the price of a new car.

You visit a car dealer and select a car for a test drive. After the drive, you go to the salesperson's cubicle in the showroom. The car has a list price of $16,000. After a short discussion, you offer $13,500, he counters with $15,600, you counter with $14,000, he counters with $15,200, you counter with $14,400, and he reduces his price to $14,800. You act as if you won't go any higher and threaten to visit another dealership. The earnest-looking salesperson then says to you: "You look like a nice person, and I can see that you really like the car. My main concern is that you get the car you want. I assume you're a reasonable person, and I want to be reasonable. How about if we split the difference—$14,600?"

The salesperson sounds fair! Why? Because 50/50 splits sound fair to most people. You might feel like an ogre if you turn this offer down. Yet logically, you should realize that this compromise, like most, is quite arbitrary. The final two numbers on the table could have been $14,000 and $14,400. Splitting these two figures would sound just as fair, but the resulting price would be $400 lower. The fairness of a 50/50 split depends on the comparative fairness of the two numbers being used as anchors. To negotiate rationally, you must be aware of the appeal of the very term "50/50 split" and realize that other 50/50 alternatives can be pulled out of a hat just as easily.

EMOTION, RATIONALITY, AND NEGOTIATION

Joe Girard is listed in the *Guiness Book of World Records* as the world's greatest car salesman. He reportedly sends out thirteen-thousand greeting cards each month to customers and potential customers. While the greeting on the front of the cards varies with the seasons, the message inside the card is always the same, simple "I like you."[5] While there are probably some other reasons for Girard's success as a salesman, the positive, friendly relationship he created with the people who got his card certainly helped. He told them he liked them, which probably made them like him.

The role of emotion or feeling, either positive or negative, remains one of the least studied areas of negotiation. Managers can begin to understand the impact of emotion on negotiation by considering what is known about the benefits of positive feelings or good humor. Psychologist Alice Isen and her colleagues have found that positive emotion is associated with greater generosity and helpfulness. It also enhances how much you like other people, improves your view of human nature and your creative problem-solving ability, and lessens your aggressiveness and hostility.[6]

One study found that how often a cocktail waitress smiled influenced her tip income. When the waitress smiled broadly, she received significantly larger tips than when she engaged her customers with weak or minimal smiles ($23.20 versus $9.40 in this study). However, positive emotion is not always associated with positive events. It can enhance the effects of biases on your judgment. For example, people who are feeling happy or content may be even more sensitive to framing, escalation of commitment, and availability effects.[7]

A couple of studies explicitly examined the impact of positive emotion on negotiator performance. Negotiators were given a small gift, thereby inducing a "good mood." In subsequent negotiations, those who were in a good mood were able to reach more creative and more integrative agreements.[8] Not only were these "happier" participants more likely to reach integrative agreements, they were less likely to use highly competitive or contentious tactics. In another study, negotiators in a positive mood rated their performance as significantly higher than those in a neutral mood, even when their performance was identical.[9] They also thought that they had done significantly better than their opponent. It seems that a positive mood can increase the need-based illusion of superiority described in Chapter 8.

THE JOINT IMPACT OF FAIRNESS AND EMOTION

Negotiations often collapse when one party becomes angry with the other and attempts to "maximize his opponent's displeasure rather than his own satisfaction."[10] How do emotions affect your perceptions of what is fair in a negotiation, and influence your decision making and subsequent behavior?

We said earlier that people tend to expect equal allocations of resources in many social and negotiation situations. However, how you allocate resources is also affected by the relationship between the parties. A manager in a long-term relationship with other parties tends to be concerned about their welfare; strangers are typically concerned with how much they get for themselves.[11]

The nature of your relationships, as well as comparisons of what an opponent gets relative to what you do, can jointly overshadow the importance of maximizing your negotiation outcome. We asked managers how satisfied they would be with different cash allocations when they had a good relationship, no relationship, or a poor relationship with the party with whom they were splitting the money.[12] While participants generally preferred equality over inequality, they also preferred advantageous inequality (when they received more than the other party), over disadvantageous inequality (when the other party received more than they did). As the relationship shifted from positive to negative, the managers became more selfish; they were more concerned with their own payoffs and much more likely to prefer advantageous inequality.

Interpersonal comparisons can also lead to irrational outcomes. We asked managers to make choices in one of three possible situations: (1) an individual, risky choice involving either gains or losses, (2) a choice in which the gains or losses (equal those in Situation 1) would be shared by the participant and someone with whom he or she had a positive relationship, and (3) the same choice as Situation 2 but with a negative relationship between the parties.[13]

In the first choice, there were two options: a sure gain of $5,000 or a risky alternative offering a 70 percent chance of $6,000 and a 30 percent chance of $4,000. In this case, 19 percent of the participants chose the sure thing and 81 percent chose the risky alternative. In the second choice, the participants had $10,000 to allocate: either $5,000 for themselves ($5,000 for the other) or a 70 percent chance of $6,000 for themselves ($4,000 for the other) and a 30 percent chance of $4,000 for themselves ($6,000 for the other). Notice that the participants' outcomes are identical in each situation. Now, however, 85 percent opted for the sure thing. When the relationship was negative, only 27 percent opted for the sure split.

When making decisions that only related to themselves, participants were willing to take risks to maximize their return. When including others in the decision, the equal split was preferred over the risky choice when the participants liked the other party. But when they had a negative relationship with the other party, participants preferred the higher-valued, risky alternative; they wanted to get as much more than the other person as they could.

Another problem examined how interpersonal comparisons affected choices involving losses. The same three situations were compared: individual, positive relationship, and negative relationship. When making a decision only for themselves, 75 percent of the participants preferred a 50/50 chance of losing $10,000 over a sure loss of $5,000 (just as we would expect from our discussion of framing in Chapter 5); however, when the choice involved another person, only 15 percent of the participants (in both the negative and positive relationships) chose the 50 percent chance of their losing $10,000 or the other party losing $10,000, while 85 percent preferred that both parties have a sure loss of $5,000 rather than both risking losing the full amount. Participants chose this option when they liked the other party because maintaining equality was important. When they didn't like the other party, participants wanted to avoid disadvantageous inequality. While this may seem inconsistent, it's easily explained by the desire for equality, using the outcome of another party in negotiation as a key reference point.

Another study we did found that in assessing a single situation, people in positive relationships care far more about how their outcome compares with the others involved than the actual value of what they got. Still, if there are different options to choose from, the comparisons become less important than the person's own outcome value.[14] For example, while 70 percent of the participants rated Outcome (1) ($400 for the participant, $400 for another person) as more acceptable than Outcome (2) ($500 for the participant, $700 for the other) when they were evaluated separately, only 22 percent actually chose (1) over (2). While outcomes of others are the reference point for evaluating separate outcomes, when there's a choice to be made, outcomes can be easily compared and individual benefits become the main evaluation criteria. Thus, the social context of various options plays a critical role in framing the negotiation.

CONCLUSIONS

Fairness and emotional considerations affect negotiation profoundly. Preferences for different standards of fairness are influenced by the emotional states of those negotiating. Negotiating rationally requires that you understand the impact of these influences on your own judgments and decisions, and that you anticipate the same influences on your opponents' behavior. Ignoring these influences makes no more sense than assuming everyone is completely rational. You must choose your rational negotiation strategies given the real emotions and concerns for fairness that everyone has.

14

Negotiating in Groups and Organizations

So far, we've focused almost exclusively on two-party negotiation; however, many negotiations occur among larger groups. Group negotiation is a process in which three or more persons, with their own interests, decide how to resolve their conflicting preferences among issues.[1] Unfortunately, what you've learned about two-party negotiation doesn't transfer to group situations readily. While in either negotiation your goal is to get the best outcome—one that integrates all interests while still best achieving your objectives—increasing the number of participants does more than just increase coordination problems. Consider the effect the power struggle between two groups had on Lehman Brothers:

Lehman Brothers, a major force on Wall Street since the 1850s, saw this dominance end when, after 134 years, the company had to be sold to avoid bankruptcy. The relationship between Lewis Gluckman, head of the trading department, and Peter Peterson, chair of the banking department, figured prominently in the company's downfall. As at many Wall Street firms, antagonism between the bankers and traders was ingrained at Lehman Brothers. On Wall Street, traders were often described by bankers as "poorly educated drones . . . thinking of the moment, not the long term," while traders stereotyped bankers as "elitist Ivy League preppies who rise late [and] take leisurely lunches."

This polarization was particularly intense at Lehman Brothers, where bankers and traders were not even housed in the same building. Although trading was historically subordinate to banking as the major source of revenue at Lehman, the trading group was now generating huge profits, further alienating the two groups. By the time Gluckman challenged Peterson for control of Lehman Brothers, the firm was more profitable than ever—due, in large part, to the income generated by the traders.

During the struggle for control, both Gluckman and Peterson looked for alliances. A core of allies formed around each man and eventually Gluckman and his coalition gained enough power to act unilaterally. They no longer put crucial decisions before the board of directors; decisions were made by the force of majority rule, with no negotiation. But Gluckman and the traders' power was short-lived. Without the normal negotiation and decision making controls, Lehman Brothers was unable to survive when the market conditions changed.[2]

Lehman Brothers suffered long-term damage because of how its employees behaved during this power struggle. Gluckman's group had enough power to force decisions that were in their best interest, but not in the organization's. Thus, while they may have thought they were following a rational strategy, Gluckman's coalition destroyed the company.

As the experience of Lehman Brothers illustrates, what may be good for one person or a coalition may be bad for the group as a whole. Shifting from negotiation between two parties to multiple parties makes it more difficult to reach rational agreement. You need to consider the varying interests of more people, which often requires that you establish coordination and decision rules, and—for the first time—you must deal with the possibility of forming coalitions. We outline prescriptions in this chapter to help you negotiate rationally in groups of any size.

MULTIPLE PARTIES, MULTIPLE INTERESTS

The dynamics of group negotiation are far more complex than those of two-party negotiations. With two parties, there are two sets of interests and one interaction. With three parties, the network grows to three sets of individual interests, three possible interactions between any two players, and one interaction of all three. In five-party situations, there are five sets of individual interests, ten possible two-player interactions, multiple potential three- and four-person subgroups, and one five-person group. This web of interests and relationships becomes increasingly complex as the numbers grow. Simply trying to coordinate all the parties' preferences and interests is a difficult undertaking.

Imagine a six-member group negotiating next year's budget. Each member has a set of interests, a reservation price, and a target. Even something so basic as determining the bargaining zone requires you to think about six reservation prices all at once. To reach an integrative agreement, you have to consider six sets of interests simultaneously as you search for solutions that work for each member as well as for the entire group.

To reduce the complexity of the amount of information there is to consider, managers often make simplifying assumptions or set up rules to follow. Unfortunately, many of these assumptions or rules work by reducing the amount of information each party learns about the other group member's true preferences. For example, groups quickly develop *norms*—rules of acceptable behavior within the group.[3] In a two-party setting, if you make what your opponent thinks is an unreasonable demand, he or she may feel justified in confronting you directly. Within a group, strong behavioral norms put greater pressure on executives to conform.[4] As the size of the group grows, you become less likely to question the group norms, regardless of the quality of agreements that result.

As we discussed in Chapter 13, people have different perceptions of what's fair in a situation. With groups, you have multiple perceptions of fairness to consider. Consequently, to help groups reach decisions, there are specific distribution rules you can follow in dividing the negotiation resources. An *equity* allocation rule divides the available resources in proportion to each group member's input.[5] *Equality* allocation rules divide the resources equally among the members. You can also divide the resources according to the *needs* of the individual group members.[6] What you've done in similar situations, or *past practice,* is also a critical way to determine the fairness of resource distributions in group negotiation.[7]

Managers in group negotiations should know not only the various norms of distribution, but the preferences of other group members. If you follow the equitable allocation rule when the other group members expect equality, it can lead to misunderstandings and inefficient outcomes. You need to be sensitive to what other group members consider fair when developing your proposals.

To resolve a negotiation, groups should agree on the appropriate allocation norm. Without the direction this norm provides, each party may follow the norm that best enhances his or her own position.[8] Alternatively, the negotiation could become anchored on an allocation rule that was chosen simply because it was the first viable norm suggested.[9]

Prescription 1: Think carefully about the distribution rule to be used in allocating resources among the parties.

Another simplifying assumption managers make about groups is that they are either *cooperative* (individual members are rewarded for group performance) or *competitive* (group members divide a fixed-sum of resources). However, most groups you work or socialize with are neither purely cooperative nor purely competitive; they are *mixed-motive.* To negotiate successfully in mixed-motive groups, members must reveal their preferences, attempt to persuade others, adopt bargaining strategies, and exchange information.

As we discussed earlier, the two primary goals of a manager in a negotiation are integration (increasing the available resources) and distribution (increasing your share of those resources). The case simulation of *The Ledger* makes clear how much harder it is to achieve these goals in groups.[10]

The Ledger is a daily morning newspaper with a circulation of 80,000. While the paper had enjoyed a reasonable profit margin on revenues of $36 million, it is now facing a decline in both circulation and advertising revenue. Fran McKay, the publisher, has asked each department head to work together on next year's strategic plan. While most of the details are resolved, three are still in dispute: capital equipment purchases; a new section aimed at elderly readers; and strategic staff additions. The heads of the business, advertising, production, circulation, and news staffs agreed to meet to resolve these issues. There are limited resources available and each department head has a different idea about what should be done.

McKay has done quite a bit of thinking about the unique interests of each department head as well as the best way to resolve these issues for the paper. To help structure the negotiation as well as to understand and reconcile the five managers' interests, McKay has created a matrix (table 14.1) of the likely values of the possible outcomes for each manager. To make it easier to compare the interests of the department heads, McKay has allocated one hundred points among the three issues for each manager. For example, Cahill, the business manager, cares a lot about the computer system and much less about the other issues. McKay has given the computer system a value of sixty points for Cahill, and assigned twenty points to each of the other issues. Each issue and each manager's interests are described below.

Capital Equipment. Cahill wants to install a system capable of computerizing all record keeping for *The Ledger*. The ideal system will provide all the necessary software to do payroll, accounts payable, the general ledger, circulation, and advertising. This system would cost $200,000. If Cahill doesn't buy the circulation software, the price can be reduced to $130,000. It can be further reduced to $40,000 by not buying the advertising software. While Cahill is really committed to computerizing the newspaper (reflected in the sixty point value), the rest of the managers don't have a big stake in this—although they would prefer to allocate the capital budget elsewhere (not buying any system is worth only ten points to each of them).

New Section. Thomas, the news department head, and Jackson, the advertising manager, strongly agree that a new weekly section targeting the elderly population would expand the paper's readership and attract a new group of advertisers. Thus, McKay has allocated them each sixty points for the section. However, the new

Table 14.1 *A Five-Party Negotiation Matrix*

The Ledger	Accounting Cahill	Circulation Chavez	News Thomas	Production Miller	Advertising Jackson
Computer System					
$200,000	60	0	0	0	0
$130,000	40	3	3	3	3
$40,000	20	6	6	6	6
No System	0	10	10	10	10
New Section					
Weekly Section	0	0	60	0	60
Biweekly Section	5	8	45	8	45
Weekly Page	10	15	30	15	30
Biweekly Page	15	23	15	23	15
No Section	20	30	0	30	0
Staffing					
N&A-8; C&P-0	20	0	30	0	30
N&A-7; C-5, P-3	17	6	27	6	27
N&A-6; C-9, P-5	15	12	24	12	24
N&A-5; C-12, P-7	12	18	21	18	21
N&A-4; C-18, P-9	9	24	18	24	18
N&A-3; C-22, P-11	6	30	15	30	15
N&A-2; C-28, P-13	3	45	7	45	7
N&A-0; C-30, P-15	0	60	0	60	0

section isn't as attractive to the circulation manager, Chavez, or to the circulation staff, as they would need to reorganize their distribution system to handle deliveries to the retirement communities around the city. Miller, manager of production, believes the additional weekly section will be more work than the staff can accommodate, although there are other options (such as a weekly or biweekly page) that are more attractive. In the business department, adding a complete new section will add more work for Cahill's already overworked staff.

Strategic Staff Additions. Because McKay is betting that people are the key to reversing the newspaper's decline, the publisher is willing to invest $500,000 in new staff from the personnel budget. This money is not related to any capital budget item. Thus, the money can be divided among each department or used by as few as two of them.

Thomas (news, N) and Jackson (advertising, A) each want to increase the size of their staffs by eight hires. If the new section becomes a reality, they want larger staffs to cover more news to attract new readers and bring in new advertisers to contribute to the paper's profitability. However, McKay thinks new staff is more important to circulation (C) and production (P). If these departments' managers were allocated the entire amount, they could hire a total of forty-five part-time employees. Thirty of the part-time employees would go to circulation to canvass the city and outlying suburbs for new subscribers, and fifteen to production to alleviate the costly overtime from the understaffed mailroom. Hiring part-time staffers will decrease the overtime of the full-time staff and produce a substantial savings for the newspaper. This value is reflected in the sixty points that McKay has allocated to Chavez and Miller if they are able to get all of the new employees. Cahill, the business manager, probably wants the paper to hire as few people as possible and would prefer full-time employees over part-time employees, but doesn't feel very strongly about this issue.

COORDINATION AND DECISION RULES: MAJORITY RULE AND AGENDAS

While many of the prescriptions that apply to integrative negotiation between two parties also apply to groups, having more than two parties makes coordination much more important. For example, has McKay set up the structure of the negotiation to insure that all of the issues are thoroughly discussed and that each party knows the preferences of the others? Is the group given sufficient time and resources for creativity in finding a solution? Is the group committed to a solution that maximizes the interests of the parties rather than reaching an agreement that is just "good enough?"

To evaluate the quality of a group-negotiated agreement in a mixed-motive context, you can use the following criteria:

1. Does the group expand its focus to include all viable negotiable issues in the discussion?
2. Does the group discuss priorities and preferences among issues?
3. Does the group focus its efforts on problem solving?
4. Will the group consider unique and innovative solutions?
5. Is the group willing to trade-off issues of high-priority interest?

Because of the complexity inherent in group negotiation, managers tend to impose rules or strategies that reduce or simplify the process required to reach agreement among group members. Unfortunately, many of these strategies limit the group's willingness or ability to explore more creative solutions—a process that is critical in meeting the five criteria listed above.

DECISION RULES: THE NORMATIVE BELIEF IN MAJORITY RULE

We've described the *Ledger* negotiation as if acceptance by all five of the managers is necessary to reach a binding agreement. While this is true in two-party negotiation, consensus in group negotiation is just one of many decision rules. Majority rule is commonly used to make decisions in groups. Whatever decision rule the group chooses can affect both the complexity of the interaction and the distribution of outcomes.

A problem that many groups face is how to determine when an agreement is reached. Groups typically rely on a rule, such as majority or unanimity, to decide when there is sufficient support for a particular outcome. While majority and unanimity are not the only methods of choice, they are among the most common.[11] Americans use majority rule—most often defined as choosing the solution that receives more than 50 percent of the votes cast—in many diverse situations. Most Americans believe majority rule to be the fairest and most efficient means of combining divergent individual preferences.[12]

Returning to table 14.1, what outcome can you expect if McKay imposes a majority rule to reach agreement for each of the issues facing the *Ledger* staff? For the computer system, the majority (four of the five managers) prefers no system; that outcome would be worth ten points to Chavez, Thomas, Miller, and Jackson. On the new section for the elderly, Cahill, Chavez, and Miller are happiest when no new section is created; that's worth twenty points to Cahill and thirty points to Chavez and Miller. On the staffing issue, Chavez and Miller would be the only two voting against letting the $500,000 in new staffing go to the news and advertising departments; Cahill would get twenty points while Thomas and Jackson would get thirty points apiece. If you then add up the total points for each manager, you find that the *majority-rule* solution would create forty points in value for each of the five parties.

Majority rule is often used because it's easy and efficient. In a purely cooperative group, it may be the *most* efficient way to reach a decision. In a purely competitive group, a majority vote may be the best way to avoid an impasse. In a mixed-motive group, however, majority rule is not so effective. When there are more than two issues to be negotiated, there are many ways majority rule can be strategically manipulated to prevent fully integrative outcomes.[13]

Majority rule fails to recognize the strengths of individual preferences. While one person may care very strongly about an issue, his or her vote counts the same as the vote of someone who doesn't have a strong opinion on that issue. For example, Cahill's vote for the $200,000 computer system counts as much as Miller's vote against the system, even though Cahill would realize six times the value should the full computer system be installed. Thus, with majority rule, group members don't have much opportunity to learn the values others place on the issues. Without this information, it's much harder to trade-off issues and find integrative agreements based on differing preferences.

What if McKay were to impose a unanimity rule? Would the results be better than the forty points each manager received under the majority rule? Studies have found that mixed-motive groups negotiating under an unanimous-decision rule reach more valuable outcomes than groups operating under majority rule.[14] As you can see from figure 14.1, if unanimity is required, the five parties could make trade-offs in their mutual best interests.

What if Cahill got the full computer system by accepting the weekly section that Thomas and Jackson want and agreeing to the forty-five new part-time hires for Chavez and Miller? Cahill's sixty points for the full computer system is clearly worth the concessions on the other two issues. Likewise, while the other four don't really care about the computer system, they each care a great deal about one of the other issues. If the final agreement among the five department heads consisted of the full computer system, a new weekly section, and forty-five new part-time employees in circulation and production, it's worth sixty points to each party—a full 50 percent better for each department head than the agreement reached by majority rule. To reach a unanimous agreement, each party has to make trade-offs that lead to an integrative outcome.

Integrative strategies require group members to learn other members' preferences and find ways to expand the pie of resources to accommodate them. While it is time-consuming, encouraging negotiation groups to reach unanimous decisions may help accomplish these goals by forcing them to consider creative alternatives to increase the pie and satisfy the interests of all group members. While majority rule is sometimes your only option, avoid it whenever you can.

Prescription 2: Avoid majority rule in group negotiations whenever possible.

AGENDAS: THE NEED FOR STRUCTURE

Groups often use agendas to organize their discussion of negotiation issues. By determining the order in which issues will be raised, discussed, and decided in the negotiation process, agendas are essential to efficient decision making. Cooperative or competitive groups typically function best when operating under agendas that keep them focused on finding the most effective decision in an orderly and efficient manner.

Typically, when agendas are followed strictly, issues are considered individually and not raised again once the group has moved on to a new topic. This may limit the exchange of information about preferences among group members and make it harder to identify new issues and find trade-offs. This doesn't matter in purely cooperative or competitive negotiations because integrative decisions aren't possible. In mixed-motive negotiation, however, groups using an agenda usually reach less integrative agreements than groups not using one because the agenda forces the group to consider the dispute on an issue-by-issue basis.[15]

In the *Ledger* negotiation, an agenda that demands that all five parties agree on each issue in turn will probably encourage each department head to see the resources available as a fixed-pie and force them into thinking in terms of simple compromise. If they decide to compromise on each of the issues, there are a number of potential agreements. Compromise A might include the $130,000 computer system, a weekly page for the elderly, and four new employees in news and advertising, eighteen in circulation, and nine in production. This would be worth fifty-nine points to Cahill; forty-two points each to Chavez and Miller; and fifty-one points each to Thomas and Jackson. In Compromise B, the parties might settle for the $40,000 computer system, a weekly page for the elderly, and five hires in news and advertising, twelve in circulation, and seven in production. This would be worth forty-two points to Cahill; thirty-nine points each to Chavez and Miller; and fifty-seven points each to Thomas and Jackson.

These possible compromises show how agendas inhibit mixed-motive groups from discussing issues simultaneously and recognizing their integrative potential. Instead of using rigid issue-oriented agendas, managers in mixed-motive groups should use agendas that structure the general problem-solving process: (1)

identify priorities, (2) reveal individual interests, and (3) suggest creative approaches to solving the problems.[16]

Prescription 3: Avoid strict issue-by-issue agendas whenever possible.

Decision rules and agendas are two options to structure group negotiation. Which particular rule the parties prefer depends on the possible outcomes achieved by using that rule. For *The Ledger,* McKay's choice should be quite clear. The integrative agreement found using the unanimity rule is worth sixty points to each department head; compromise agreements will tend to be worth less than sixty points for each of the parties; and the majority rule outcome is worth only forty points to each member of the group.

Prescription 4: Focus on the differing interests and preferences of group members to facilitate creative integrative agreements.

COALITIONS AND GROUP NEGOTIATIONS

Perhaps the most fundamental difference between two-party and group negotiations is the potential for two or more parties within a group to form a coalition in order to pool their resources and have a greater influence on outcomes. The traders at Lehman Brothers formed a coalition with power enough to allocate resources for their own short-term gains, to the disadvantage of other individuals, groups, and the overall organization.

Ideally, a group decision should be made with all members focusing on the same objective. Unfortunately, members frequently focus on their own interests and those of their particular coalition. Those outside the coalition may be less effective and less productive because they have access to fewer resources. At Lehman Brothers, what was best for one coalition was clearly not in the best interest of the organization.

Another reason coalitions can influence group outcomes is that they involve fewer people and are therefore easier to manage. Coordination problems are reduced, the interests and goals of members are more consistent, and motivating them to act is easier. This gives the coalition an edge over the other group members. Instead of putting in the time, effort, and creativity required to reach an integrative agreement among the group, those in a powerful coalition can get what they want using majority rule.

While majority rule can be an efficient way to determine how to divide resources, in mixed-motive groups where coalitions have formed, it can easily lead to outcomes that are not in the larger group's best interests. Research has found that when group members had equal power, the group achieved more integrative agreements and used resources more effectively than groups where coalitions formed and power was distributed unevenly.[17] Furthermore, in groups already suffering from power imbalances, group members were much more likely to form coalitions to take advantage of that imbalance.

In the *Ledger* negotiation, there are many opportunities for coalitions to form among the five department heads. One possible three-way coalition would consist of Cahill, Thomas, and Jackson. Cahill would trade a promise of support for the weekly section (worth sixty points to Thomas and Jackson), for their support of the $200,000 computer system (worth sixty points to Cahill). This is not a stable situation. Think about what you would do if you were Chavez (circulation) or Miller (production). With Cahill, Thomas, and Jackson in a coalition, your outcome looks poor. Since they already agree on the computer system and the new section, the only issue left is new staffing, one that you care a great deal about. If the coalition holds, then you probably aren't going to get the forty-five new part-time staff members you need. So, it's now in your best interest to go to Cahill and offer to support the full computer system and kill the new section (a deal worth eighty points to Cahill) in exchange for Cahill's support on hiring forty-five part-time employees.

Now, Thomas and Jackson are out of the coalition and face a very poor outcome. What's to stop them from trying to commit Chavez or Miller to a new coalition by promising a better deal than either might get from their current coalition? This can go on indefinitely. Of course, while all of this politicking is going on, McKay is probably having problems getting the newspaper out.

To reach better outcomes in both the Lehman Brothers and the *Ledger* cases, managers should first structure the negotiation to require consensus rather than majority rule. Second, managers should emphasize finding outcomes that are beneficial for the group as well as the individual, balancing short- and long-term interests and benefits for all group members.

Prescription 5: Recognize that coalitions are inherently unstable, often leading to agreements that are not in the best interest of the organization.

CONCLUSIONS

In this chapter we've covered a broad spectrum of issues about multiparty negotiation. As we mentioned in the chapter introduction, group negotiations are inherently more complex than two-party situations. This is due, in part, to the richness of the interpersonal networks and the multiple individual preferences and interests involved.

We described how group negotiations are more difficult than two-party negotiations: the increased number of people and interests require managers to establish coordination and decision rules and lead to the risk of coalitions, which usually allocate resources ineffectively. Group negotiations are becoming increasingly common in and among organizations. To effectively manage these negotiations, you need to look more carefully for integrative opportunities, be aware of barriers to integrative agreements, and be sensitive to the impact of decision rules on the quality of group outcomes. Negotiating as a group allows you to take advantage of the knowledge, information, and perspective of each member to reach a creative, integrative solution. The trick here is not to let yourself miss out on those benefits by only looking for the quick and easy answers.

15

Negotiating Through Third Parties

You've probably been part of negotiations that include a third party—someone who is not a negotiator per se. While a third party might not care about the exact nature of the final outcome, he or she *is* interested in your reaching an agreement. What effect do third parties have on agreements in negotiation?

Consider how the third party, a real estate agent, affects your decision in the following situation:

You want to buy a house. You and your real estate agent looked at potential homes for the last two months and you're about to make an offer. (Of course, you have two other properties in mind, as we suggested in Chapter 9!) The listing price on this house is $199,500. After talking it over with your agent, you decide to offer $160,000. Almost immediately, the owner counters with an offer of $189,000, which the agent delivers to you at your apartment. While sitting in your kitchen, you say you want to take some time to think about your next move. The agent is adamant that it is not the right strategy. He has a contract ready for you to sign with your next offer—all you have to do is decide what the numbers are. He says it really doesn't matter what you offer, but you should make a counteroffer soon.

Your agent is very knowledgeable about real estate and the local market. You have to decide whether you should listen to him and make an immediate counteroffer or take some time to think about it. What would you do?

When negotiating through third parties, such as a real estate agent, you need to know not only what's important to you, but what's important to the third party as well. In this chapter, we consider the third-party roles of mediator, arbitrator, and agent in negotiation. We also look at the third-party roles managers play. Understanding the role played in a negotiation by any type of third party helps you choose more rational strategies. (We return to you, the realtor, and the kitchen later in the chapter.)

A *mediator* in negotiation helps the parties come to an agreement, but cannot impose a settlement on them. Mediation is often used to settle labor disputes. An *arbitrator* lets the parties present their own sides of the dispute, then imposes the solution, as in baseball salary disputes. *Agents,* such as real estate agents, usually represent one of the parties, and are primarily interested in their own outcomes. Unlike the other third-party roles, agents typically have a vested interest in getting not just an agreement, but the best agreement that increases their own share of the pie.

Managers are unique as third parties because they aren't restricted in what they can do in the way formal mediators, arbitrators, or agents are. Managers can choose options ranging from ignoring the dispute to telling the arguing parties just what the solution will be (and anything in between).

Whether you think of third parties as neutral or interested players in a negotiation, remember that they are part of the negotiation and, as such, you need to consider their interests, incentives, and influence. Knowing what motivates a third party can provide you with the insight needed to negotiate more rationally.

While third parties can often help find agreements in negotiations where impasse seemed inevitable, involving a third party does have its costs. A third party may exert considerable pressure on all sides to agree; it can be difficult to stand up to such pressure, even when you're being urged to agree to something that's not in your best interest. The goal of this chapter is to point out the ways you can best use third parties to help you reach high-quality agreements.

NEGOTIATING THROUGH MEDIATORS

Mediators facilitate negotiation agreements by controlling how the parties interact. They can also help put together an agreement, but the parties decide whether to accept it. While mediation is a popular intervention strategy, it is not a panacea. It doesn't work well if the parties are really hostile. Mediators can often help parties make concessions and reach agreement in negotiations over minor conflicts of interest, but they aren't as effective when the conflict is large, there's a lot at stake, or the differences are perceived to be substantial.[1]

Because mediators focus on getting the parties to agree, they're sometimes criticized for not being concerned with getting an agreement that's in the best interests of one or both sides. While you may want a mediator to help you get a good agreement, the mediator's incentive is to reach an agreement, *any* agreement. Because an impasse is sometimes better than any available agreement if you are negotiating through a mediator, you must be able to decide when accepting an agreement is best for you or whether it's wiser to walk away without one.[2]

This isn't always easy because the presence of a third party can change the way the parties in a negotiation interact. In divorce mediation, for example, each side usually perceives what the mediator does as more crucial to a successful outcome than either the actual dispute or the parties' own characteristics.[3] Because a mediator has such an impact, it's important that you always remember that simply reaching an agreement is the goal for most mediators. Yet, what you want is a mediator who will increase your chances of getting the most integrative agreement when there's a positive bargaining zone, and an *impasse* when there's a negative bargaining zone.

Unfortunately, mediation won't usually meet your ideal. Most mediators influence the dispute resolution process by not only fashioning agreements, but by convincing the parties to agree to them. For instance, in a negotiation between parties when one is clearly more powerful than the other, the mediator's goal of reaching an agreement makes possible three strategies. The mediator can try to get both parties to make similar concessions, get the more powerful party to concede, or get the weaker party to concede.

Any of these strategies will probably work. The mediator may take the path of least resistance and get the weaker party to make the concessions. In doing so, mediators may compromise that party's interests by suggesting concessions that are clearly one-sided, just to get an agreement. Alternatively, if mediators want to equalize power, they may try to get the more powerful party to concede. Or if the goal is compromise, they may extract equal, and not necessarily rational, concessions from each party.

Professional mediators disagree about these multiple goals in determining their role as third parties. But whichever strategy mediators choose, they are quite adept at selecting goals that will foster agreement using whatever tools or arguments necessary to persuade the contending parties to accept it.

NEGOTIATING THROUGH ARBITRATORS

Arbitration differs from mediation in that the arbitrator determines the final outcome. How arbitrators make that decision depends on the type of arbitration used. In conventional arbitration, the final agreement is based on the arguments and positions of the conflicting parties, with the arbitrator usually selecting an agreement that falls between their final positions.[4] Often, conventional arbitrators are accused of simply splitting the difference between the parties' final offers.

If the arbitrator does, in fact, split this difference, how might you behave in a negotiation that could go to arbitration? You could resist making any concessions so that if arbitration is imposed the final position will be relatively closer to your position than to your opponent's. On the surface, this seems to be an incentive for parties *not* to concede (or concede less). This behavior, paradoxically, causes many more negotiations to end up in arbitration because the parties are unwilling to make concessions to reach an agreement for fear of going to arbitration with weakened or compromised positions.[5]

Final-offer arbitration was introduced as an answer to this problem. Under final-offer arbitration, the arbitrator has to choose one or the other of the parties' final offers, and thus, has little control over designing the agreement. As we described in Chapter 8, this is often used to resolve professional baseball salary disputes between players and owners. As you might guess, negotiating parties reach agreements on their own more often when they face final-offer arbitration than when they face conventional arbitration. Knowing there's more to lose if the other side's final position is chosen by the arbitrator, the parties are more willing to make concessions in the negotiation to reach their own solution.[6]

The strategy you use to negotiate through arbitrators depends on the type of arbitration. In conventional arbitration, you need to educate and persuade the arbitrator with information favorable to your side. One strategy is to use some of the decision biases we've discussed previously to influence the arbitrator; however, if you try to benefit from these biases without careful consideration, it can lead to absurd behavior. For instance, if you're trying to anchor the arbitrator's assessment of a fair outcome, you may try to justify an excessively high or low offer. This is akin to trying to buy a house that is listed for $300,000 by offering $0 (to anchor the other side) and assuming that you will end up with a sale at $150,000 by splitting the difference between the two positions. What happens is what we warned about in Chapter 4: your offer will not be considered seriously because an offer must be credible to be accepted as an anchor. To anchor an arbitrator's decisions, you have to persuade him or her that not only is your offer fair, but so is your reasoning. One way to convince the arbitrator of the benefits of your offer is to frame outcomes favorable to you as gains for the other side.

If you are facing final-offer arbitration, you need to persuade the arbitrator that your final offer is fair. To do this, you need to understand not only the arbitrator's notion of what is fair, but predict (accurately) what your opponent will propose. With this information, you can then propose a final offer that will seem fairer to the arbitrator than your opponent's will.

Again you must remember the importance of considering the thoughts and potential behavior of others. Beyond knowing how the arbitrator thinks, you have to consider how your opponent is likely to behave (both before and during arbitration). What will influence your opponent's decision to reach an agreement instead of invoking arbitration?

Another bias, the availability of information as described in Chapter 6, can also influence an agreement. Information about the costs associated with arbitration plays a big role in the parties' willingness to reach an agreement. When the costs of invoking final-offer arbitration are clear and substantial, negotiators are much more likely to reach a negotiated agreement. In addition, the threat of final-offer arbitration leads negotiators to resolve more issues and be more concessionary than the threat of conventional arbitration.[7]

Because the arbitration process requires each party to make concrete choices, it's an ideal context for studying the decisions of parties in dispute resolution. This can help you better understand how the parties and the arbitrator think about negotiation so you can develop strategies to achieve more rational, efficient outcomes.

NEGOTIATING THROUGH AGENTS

Although mediators and arbitrators are typically uninterested in the particulars of the final agreement, agents have a vested interest in the outcome because they formally represent one of the parties. While you'd like your agent to have your interests at heart, this is not always the case (especially when your interests are different from the factor on which the agent's commission or pay is based). Many sports agents, for example, see their role as "looking after the interests of the players."[8] However, consider the case of sports agents Norby Walters and Lloyd Bloom.

In August, 1988, an eight-count indictment for racketeering, mail fraud, and conspiracy to commit extortion was handed down against Norby Walters and his partner, Lloyd Bloom. These agents allegedly offered college football players clothing, concert and airline tickets, automobiles, cash, interest-free loans, hotel accommodations, use of limousines, insurance policies, trips to entertainment events, introductions to celebrities, and cash to their families. In return, the agents got at least forty-three athletes to sign postdated contracts for the agents' exclusive rights to represent the players when they turned pro. These contracts were made to look as if they were signed after the players had completed their last year of eligibility, as NCAA rules expressly prohibit players from signing such contracts before then.

When some of these same players tried to get out of the contracts, the agents purportedly threatened at least four of them, saying they'd see to it that the athletes never played football again. In addition, Bloom is accused of defrauding Paul Palmer, the Kansas City Chiefs running back, by convincing Palmer to invest nearly one third of his $450,000 signing bonus in a "credit repair" business, after which Bloom used the money to lease a Rolls-Royce and pay off $7,000 in clothing bills, as well as his credit cards bills, his ex-wife's rent, and karate classes.[9]

Theoretically, agents act for, on behalf of, or as representatives of disputants or clients.[10] Like mediators, they may have little power to impose a solution. On the other hand, they often have considerably more information about a negotiation than one or both of the parties involved, and they don't always use this information to promote the interests of their clients. Even honest agents typically have incentives that are at odds with those of their clients. Thus agents can act against the interests of one or both of the parties in a dispute.

Agents are used in negotiation because of their specialized knowledge. In a common dispute, such as one involving a buyer, a residential real-estate agent, and a seller, the agent knows about the housing market, and has special skills to identify and match prospective buyers and sellers. Sometimes the agent is passive, simply acting as the messenger between the buyer and seller; other times, the agent may be more active, even to the point of directly participating in forming an agreement.

Agents must be compensated by one or both parties. That's why the bargaining zone in a direct negotiation between buyer and seller is reduced when an agent is involved. While the potential buyer and seller both depend upon the agent(s) to represent them, legally the agent is usually responsible only to the seller, regardless of the agent-buyer relationship. Because the seller pays the agent's commission, based on the selling price of the property, the agent has a clear incentive to be biased in favor of the seller's interests. This may influence the way the agent shares information with each party.

The agent's commission usually increases the sales price of a piece of property because the seller wants to pay the commission out of the surplus created by the sale. The amount of the increase can be unclear. It could be simply the amount of the agent's commission; however, once the agent feels sure of an agreement, he or she has an incentive to push the price as high as the buyer will accept to increase the commission. This increase in price could create more than enough surplus to cover the commission; the rest is added profit for the seller.

Realtors commonly use this type of argument to convince sellers to list with an agent instead of trying to sell their home by themselves. Still, there is also an objective market value for the house that has nothing to do with how the property is sold. That value (and consequently the selling price) should not change if an agent is involved.

These two perspectives on agents lead to very different conclusions: either the buyer ends up paying the agent's commission through a higher selling price or the seller incurs this cost because the true value of the house is dictated by the market, not the agent, seller, or buyer.

In our research, we've directly compared the selling price of a house and impasse rates to see the effects of transactions using no third party, an agent, and a mediator.[11] Selling prices *and* impasse rates were higher with agent-assisted negotiations than in negotiations with no third party.

You probably already know that using an agent is costly. If you're the seller, however, and the agent helps you form an agreement that increases your surplus, then the agent may be worth the cost. If you're either the buyer or the seller, you need to decide how much information to share with your agent. Is it in your best interest to tell the agent your reservation price, for instance? Or would you do better by keeping that information to yourself? We found that the selling price was lowest when the agent knew only the seller's reservation price. When the agent knew only the buyer's reservation price, he or she used it to inflate the selling price and earn more money. The highest impasse rate occurred when the agent knew both parties' reservation prices.[12] Thus, it's best for sellers if the agent knows just the buyer's reservation price or both the buyer's and seller's reservation prices.

It is essential to consider the decision-making processes and incentive structures of various types of third parties. Executives can maximize their interests in a negotiation if they rationally consider all the available information concerning *every* party at the table.

MEANWHILE, BACK IN THE KITCHEN

Now, back to our opening story. Given what you now know about the incentives of real estate agents, should you take the advice of your agent and make an immediate counteroffer? Our answer is "no." Think carefully about what your agent wants: to get you and the seller to reach an agreement. If he realizes half of the typical 6 percent of commission (the other half of the commission usually goes to his real estate company), each additional thousand dollars of profit is worth only $30 to him. However, your agent won't push you too hard on price if he thinks you'll walk away. It's better for him if you stay in the bidding; the final price is less important than getting an agreement. At a selling price of $170,000, he receives $5,100. At a selling price of $180,000, he receives $5,400. However, if there's no agreement, he receives nothing.

By getting you to make a second bid, the agent gets you to escalate your commitment to reaching an agreement. The agent wants to maintain the momentum because it increases the probability that you'll be willing to make future price concessions. In the excitement and uncertainty of the process, you can easily lose sight of your goal of getting this house for a fair price to just getting this house (almost regardless of price). The closer the agent can get your bid to the other party's, the easier it will be for one of you to accept a compromise. "We're only a couple of thousand dollars apart, let's just split the difference and call it a deal!" Once you realize that the agent's primary goal is to get you to reach an agreement, you are better prepared to use the agent's behavior to create your own successful negotiation strategy.

NEGOTIATING THROUGH MANAGERS

Mediators, arbitrators, and agents are found in many negotiation settings; their options for intervening in any dispute are limited by the definition of their roles. In organizations, managers are often called on to resolve a variety of conflicts. Managers are not confined to using predetermined third-party roles to find agreements; they can use many different strategies when intervening in disputes among their peers and subordinates.[13]

Managers using mediation as a strategy are different from formal mediators because managers are often personally involved in the conflict. They're not only interested in the specifics of how the dispute is resolved, but they often must consider the interests of the organization and the disputants. Unlike most other third-party intervenors, managers have an ongoing relationship with the parties in the negotiation that typically begins prior to the dispute and continues after it's resolved.

As a result of their unique positions (vis-à-vis their subordinates), they can select from a wide variety of intervention strategies. Managers can ignore the dispute, choose to mediate, or even impose a settlement unilaterally (arbitration). They can let the parties try to solve the problem and step in to impose a solution only if it become clear that the parties will not or cannot agree. Thus, the manager's behavior is best described as a marriage of multiple-intervention strategies.

When negotiating through informal third parties like managers, you need to understand how to influence their behavior. Do you know when your manager will choose not to intervene in a dispute; when they will mediate; and when they will impose a solution? While it may be partially true that managers choose strategies that maximize their control of the outcome, it's not the full story. There are five important factors that influence a manager's choice of intervention style: his or her goals for the intervention; amount of conflict; how important the conflict is; time pressure; and the relative power of the manager and the disputants.

How managers intervene is influenced by their *goals*. One group of managers surveyed was less concerned with fairness as a goal, but much more concerned with efficiency, than a group of nonmanagers. Those most concerned with efficiency try to have the most control over the actual outcome. Those who want the disputants to implement the eventual solution step back and let the parties play a major role in determining it.[14]

When managers are third parties to an organizational dispute, they may have multiple, opposing goals. For example, they may want to resolve the dispute efficiently as well as assure that the eventual solution is accepted. The strategies needed to achieve these conflicting goals may change over time or require more or less control depending on the relative importance of the goals during the negotiation.

How managers intervene also depends on the *amount of conflict* they expect. If the parties appear to be close to resolving the dispute, managers may not get involved or will do so in ways that minimize their impact.[15]. If the parties appear far apart, managers may choose more controlling strategies, especially if they want to be the final authority for solving disputes or if the parties are not likely to work together again.

The *importance* of the dispute is critical. Managers need to take more care and control of the outcome if the dispute affects the organization significantly. If the dispute is peripheral to the organization, then the manager may just focus on how the dispute is resolved and use less intrusive strategies, such as helping the parties reach their own agreement.

Managers facing serious deadlines are more interested in getting a settlement. Their interventions become more aggressive as the deadlines draw closer and *time pressure* increases.[16]

The relative power of the disputants and the third party is also very important. Managers must consider who the disputants are when deciding how to intervene. When the parties are subordinates, managers intervene in a more controlling manner than when they are peers or superiors.[17] In cases where managers are called on to intervene in disputes among their superiors or peers, they are more likely to try to mediate those disputes.

The hierarchical position of the manager also has a big impact. The higher managers are in the organization, the more likely they are to share power and authority with their subordinates, which the subordinates prefer. In addition, those higher in the organization prefer less formal intervention by their managers than lower-ranking employees do. Thus, at different levels, managers and disputants prefer different intervention procedures. Lower-ranking employees may be more concerned with fairness and impartiality; higher-ranking employees may care more about controlling the actual outcome. The difference in levels of knowledge of various employees and managers also affects the intervention strategies used. Higher-ranking employees may know as much about their work as their superiors and therefore want more autonomy in their decision making.[18]

CONCLUSIONS

The central point of this chapter is that when negotiating through third parties, you need to consider their goals, interests, and likely behavior in order to develop effective strategies. Third parties are rarely completely neutral judges of what is best for you. You need to remember that the third party is an active participant in the negotiation process—a participant who has vested interests in particular outcomes.

Managers who are the third party in a negotiation must be very flexible. You should be able to adjust the intensity of your intervention strategies from inaction to complete control. The uncertainty of deciding which strategy to use under which circumstances makes this more difficult. But the best preparation for this third-party role, and for working with managers who are the third parties in your own negotiations, is to know the managers or disputants, their incentives, constituency demands, and goals.

CHAPTER
16

Competitive Bidding
The Winner's Curse Revisited

Dave Barry, the very funny, and often strange, columnist recently wrote about the peculiar things people will do for money and to be on TV.[1] Based on people's willingness to be on and watch programs about unusual personal and bodily problems, Barry proposed a new television show entitled "Eat Bugs For Money." On the show, a large live insect would be brought out, and contestants would secretly write down the minimum amount of money they'd take to eat the bug. The lowest bidder ("the winner") would then eat the bug and get that amount of money. Barry claimed that the idea came from his editor, who publicly stated that he would eat a "live South Florida cockroach (average weight: 11 pounds)" for $20,000. Barry's wife offered to eat the cockroach for just $2,000. Barry closed the article by asking readers who were interested in beating her offer to drop him a line. Before you read on, guess the lowest price Barry received in response.

In this chapter, we explore the competitive bidding problem. The strategies we describe could help Barry minimize his payouts on the bug-eating auction and explain why he could pay far *less* than you might think for people to eat these disgusting creatures. But before we analyze Barry's bug bids, consider a more usual side of competitive bidding.

Organizations frequently bid against competitors for employees or other valued resources such as contracts, patents, or other firms. In such competitive bidding, each party wants their bid to be the

winning offer. Limited interaction and antitrust laws often provide little opportunity for communication between the competing
parties. Consider the following scenarios:

Your baseball team is bidding on a free agent—a hitter with
an erratic, although sometimes outstanding, record. In the
free agent draft, eleven teams (including yours) draft the
player and appear interested in negotiating for his services.
After discussions with each of these teams, the player accepts
your offer as the most lucrative for him. Is the player going to
be worth your team's investment?

As the owner of a small movie theater, you must bid
against a number of other theaters for the rights to show
first-run films. There's a film scheduled for release in six
months that's expected to be very successful. Along with the
other theater owners, you have to bid for the movie without
seeing it. You make a bid; it's high enough to "beat" your
nearby competitors and win you the right to show the movie
in your theater. Is it time to celebrate?

Your conglomerate is considering acquiring a new firm.
Many other firms are also bidding for it. The target firm,
whose actual value is very uncertain, suggests they will gladly
be acquired by the highest bidder. You bid on the target. Of
the half dozen firms who also bid, your bid is the highest and
you acquire the target. Have you been successful?

You're attending an art auction and are very attracted to a
particular piece. You don't want to pay more than it's worth,
but you think that it is quite valuable. While you realize you
have limited expertise, you think the many bidders also in the
auction confirm that this piece of art is valuable. You win the
auction. Should you be happy?

In each of these competitive situations, a naive analysis would
suggest that you should be happy you won. You got what you
wanted at a price you set. However, it's more likely that you've
fallen victim to the "winner's curse" in competitive bidding.[2]
The winner's curse in competitive bidding is conceptually
related to the winner's curse in negotiation. In a two-party
negotiation, the winner's curse results when you fail to consider

the perspective of the other side, usually the seller. In competitive bidding, the winner's curse occurs when the winning bidder doesn't consider the implications of bidding higher than a large number of other bidders, all of whom have the same information disadvantage as the winning bidder, relative to the seller.

One reason you were the highest bidder in each scenario might be that you significantly overestimated the actual value of the commodity being sold.[3] Try the following experiment on your friends or co-workers (the more people the better). Fill a jar with coins, making note of the amount of money you put in. Now auction off the jar (offering to pay the winning bidder in dollar bills to control for "penny aversion"[4]). You're likely to get these results: the average bid will be significantly less than the value of the coins (people are trying to make money), but the winning bid will significantly *exceed* the amount of money in the jar. The winning bidder has voluntarily offered to pay an amount that loses money for him or her, and is profitable to you. Why would anyone bid more than the true value of the money?

This experiment was run forty-eight times on different groups of MBA students (twelve different classes participated in four auctions).[5] Students were shown jars containing $8 in coins and were asked to estimate each jar's value before the jars were then auctioned off to the highest bidder. Also, a $2 prize was offered for the closest guess. While the students' estimates of the value were biased downward—the mean guess across all forty-eight experiments was $5.13, well below the $8 value—we didn't lose any money. The average winning auction bid in forty-eight auctions was $10.01, producing an average loss to the "winner" of $2.01.

Figure 16.1 provides a graphic depiction of what occurred. Curve E shows the distribution of bidder estimates for the true value of the commodity, and curve B depicts the distribution of bids. The depiction assumes (1) that the mean of the distribution is equal to the true value of the commodity; i.e., no aggregate under- or overestimation is expected; and (2) that bidders take a fixed amount off their estimates to make their bids—which explains the leftward shift of the estimate distribution. The figure suggests that a winning bid (i.e., one from the right tail of the distribution) will probably exceed the actual value of the commodity. The highest bidder is usually one of the highest estimators. With no reason to believe that he or she has better information

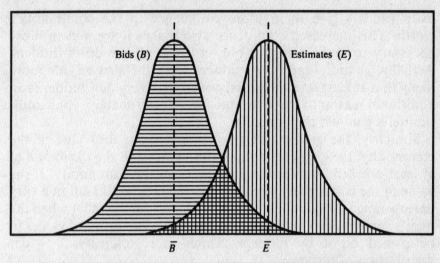

Figure 16.1 describes a graph. The axes are unlabeled except for the two curves:

Bids (*B*) and Estimates (*E*), with marks $\bar{B}$ and $\bar{E}$ below.

Variables	Assumptions
E = Estimates *B* = Bid *D* = (Amount of discounting) = *E-B*	1. True value = $\bar{E}$ 2. True value will be equal for all bidders

Figure 16.1   Graphic Illustration of the Winner's Curse

SOURCE: M. H. Bazerman and W. F. Samuelson, "I Won the Auction but Don't Want the Prize; *Journal of Conflict Resolution, 27,* pp. 618–34. Copyright © 1983 by Sage Publications, Inc. Reprinted by permission of Sage Publications, Inc.

than the other bidders, the "winner" overpays in winning the auction. A general conclusion is that *the "winner" in auctions with many bidders for commodities of highly uncertain value is really a loser who commonly pays more than the commodity is worth.*[6]

To avoid falling prey to the winner's curse in competitive bidding, remember that if you think your bid will win the auction, you may have overestimated the value of the commodity in comparison to other bidders.[7] If you're competing against many other bidders for a commodity of highly uncertain value, you should lower both your estimate of the true value of the commodity and your bid. If you do win, you're less likely to overbid, and if you do overbid, at least it will be by a smaller margin.

Your chance of losing, and the magnitude of the loss, in a competitive bidding situation increases with the number of bidders and your uncertainty about the value of the commodity.[8] Most people raise their bids as the number of parties increases;

extra bidders give them more confidence in the commodity's worth. This increased confidence also makes it seem even more necessary to make a higher bid and beat all the other bidders. Actually, as more and more bidders enter the auction, it's more likely that at least one will grossly overbid. Every new bidder is an additional reason to leave the auction. Unfortunately, your intuition tells you just the opposite.

Similarly, the greater the uncertainty about the value of the commodity, the greater the range of the bids and the likelihood of at least one bid far exceeding the value of the commodity. If the value of the commodity were certain, the bids would fall in a very narrow range. Auctions obviously work best for the seller when the item's value is more subjective, allowing a wider range of values to be placed on it by bidders, which in turn creates a wider distribution of responses.

The winner's curse has also been studied in low-bid auctions, where multiple firms are bidding for a project, and the lowest bid wins the contract (similar to Barry's bug auction).[9] In one study, the participants were a group of construction firm managers who take part in low-bid auctions all the time. Their experience in low-bid auctions raised the question of whether their experience would generalize to this context, allowing them to make more rational decisions. The winner's curse prevailed. The managers did no better than student participants, bidding lower than the actual costs of the contracts. They lacked the expertise to generalize their knowledge and auction experience to even the very similar context of the study.

APPLICATIONS

The winner's curse was first identified in the oil industry. Three engineers from Atlantic Richfield, E. C. Capen, R. V. Clapp, and W. M. Campbell, observed that:

> In recent years, several major companies have taken a rather careful look at their record and those of the industry in areas where sealed competitive bidding is the method of acquiring leases. The most notable of these areas, and perhaps the most interesting, is the Gulf of Mexico. Many analysts turn up with

the rather shocking result that, while there seems to be a lot of oil and gas in the region, the industry is not making as much return on its investments as intended. In fact, if one ignores the era before 1950, when land was a good deal cheaper, he finds that the Gulf has paid off at something less than the local credit union.[10]

They cite a number of studies to support their claim, and document the interesting finding that the ratio between the highest and lowest bids by serious bidders is commonly as high as 5:1 (and in rare cases as high as 100:1). One example is the 1969 bidding on the Alaska North Slope, where the winning bid was $900 million and the second highest bid was only $370 million. The winning bidder could have comfortably bid $500 million less and still won.

Capen, Clapp, and Campbell published their conclusions in 1971, before all of the results were in on the 1,223 leases issued in the Gulf of Mexico. Since then, other researchers have followed up this issue. One group of researchers reported that "for all 1,223 leases, firms suffered an average present value loss of $192,128 per lease . . . 62% of all leases in our data base were dry. . . . Another 16% of the leases were unprofitable. . . . Only 22% of the leases were profitable, and these leases earned only 18.74%."[11] Thus, it seems the winner's curse prevailed.

The winner's curse is also found in the competitive bidding in corporate takeovers. Why do firms pay substantially more than market price to acquire other firms? The popular answer is synergy, but there's no evidence that the synergy created has warranted the premiums paid. As many as one-third of all acquisitions prove to be failures; an additional one-third fail to live up to expectations.[12] In addition, research suggests that while stockholders of target firms make significant profits when their firms are purchased, there is no gain for the acquirers.[13] The acquirers' erroneous decisions are nicely described in the following: "In each situation, the acquirers overestimated the present value of the target to the acquirer. The acquirers did not obtain sufficient information or properly evaluate the information obtained; hunch was substituted for analysis. The fear of competitive offers justified their willingness to accept less information than they would have liked, and resulted in the acquirers increasing their bids beyond those likely with more complete information."[14]

Acquirers make their own assessments of the value of the target firm, and often trust those estimates more than they trust the market.[15] Despite everyone's fallible judgment and the widespread knowledge that acquirers don't make money in the acquisition process, bidding continues based on the executives' overconfidence in their own judgments. As a result, the firm that most overestimates the value of the target firm is the one most likely to acquire it—and suffer the winner's curse. Potential acquirers should temper their optimism by recognizing that the winning bidder is likely to pay a far greater price than the target is actually worth.

Similar conclusions can be reached in many other industries. In the publishing industry, for example, it's very common for multiple publishers in the trade book market to bid on the same proposed work. One important factor in the bidding is the advance that the author receives. One study concluded that, for publishers, "The problem is, simply, that most of the auctioned books are not earning their advances. In fact, very often such books turned out to be dismal failures whose value was more perceived than real."[16] Of course, (over)confidence leads every author to expect that his or her own book won't be in that category.

A final application of the winner's curse in auction contexts comes from the world of baseball.[17] Not surprisingly, research has found that baseball teams bidding for free agents pay more than the true worth of the player. Our earlier arguments predict that teams would overpay most when many other teams were bidding and each had diverse opinions about the player's worth. Team owners seem to have realized the costs of the winner's curse, and responded with the tactic of collusion. For some period of time, the teams stopped bidding on other teams' players. Unfortunately for the team owners, they were found guilty of illegal collusion in the 1986–87 off-season and were forced to make restitution to the players. They've since resumed their loss-making competitive bidding practices.

CONCLUSIONS

"Winning bidders" often find they've overpaid for the commodities they've bought. This happens because the highest bid is likely to be from a person or a company with a more optimistic estimate of the commodity's value than others bidding. Because most bidders don't realize this, they end up actually losing in competitive bidding contexts, even if they've "won" what they bid on. Many managers respond by arguing that their business requires that they take part in competitive bidding. We argue that being aware of the winner's curse should allow a manager to select more carefully the situations to bid in, anticipate the influence of many bidders, and realize the value of having accurate information about the worth of the commodity under consideration. Much like the value of an independent appraisal, as we discussed in Chapter 7, an independent and unbiased assessment of the value of the commodity up for auction can be critically important. The added complexity of multiple bidders makes negotiating rationally more complex and more important to understand. "Winning" the auction is clearly not always the victory that it appears to be.

And what about Dave Barry's bug auction? Barry tells us that he received many offers that beat his wife's bid to eat the "live South Florida cockroach (average weight: 11 pounds)." In fact, many bidders even offered to do it for free![18] While this is inconsistent with the expectations many of us hold about bug-eating, it is very consistent if you understand the winner's curse in an auction context. When lots of people are bidding on a "prize" of uncertain value, the winner should expect that prize to be worth less than the winning bid. In low-bid auctions like Barry's, the lowest bidder can expect to win at a price below the actual cost or value of what was won. The "prize" of eating a bug makes the meaning of the winner's curse quite clear!

CHAPTER

17

Negotiating
Through Action

You don't always have the luxury of negotiating face-to-face. Instead, you often negotiate with other parties through your actions. This can create problems. There are times when behavior that is rational for one person leads to outcomes that are irrational for the larger group, or society.

This is illustrated by the classic problem of a group of herdsmen who graze their cattle in a shared pasture of commons.[1] Each herdsman knows that if he increases the size of his herd, he increases his personal profit. The cost of grazing, measured by the damage done to the commons, is shared by all of the herdsmen. If the total number of animals gets too large, the pasture will be overgrazed and eventually destroyed. Thus, it's in the herdsmen's *collective* interest to establish individual limits on the total number of cattle grazing in the commons so that the pasture is used at a rate at which it can replenish itself. At the same time, it's in each herdsman's *individual* interest to increase the size of his herd beyond his limit. Most herdsmen respond to the short-term incentive and increase the size of their herds—leading to the ultimate destruction of the commons.[2] What would you do?

It's easy to draw a parallel between this dilemma and many of the broader resource-scarcity and pollution issues that society faces today. The dilemma is also reflected in the choices that competitors face in the marketplace. In each of these situations, the parties communicate only through their actions. The herdsmen indicate their level of cooperation not by announcing it, but by how many cattle they graze. This behavior is usually more prevalent when laws prevent face-to-face negotiation (antitrust laws are an example), and when little trust exists between the parties. Consider this type of negotiation in a simple two-party context.

> You are a product manager in charge of marketing a liquid dishwasher detergent. You have only one significant competitor in the liquid dishwasher detergent market. You must decide whether or not to put on an advertising campaign that gives consumers negative information about your competitor's product, such as the destructive impact that the liquid dishwasher detergent has on the dishwasher's motor, spots left on the dishes, etc.
>
>   Unfortunately, the other company is simultaneously thinking about advertising the negative aspects of your product. Thus, the future profitability of your product depends not only on the decision you make, but also on the decision the other company makes. Specifically, if neither firm puts on the negative ads, each firm will make $1 million profit for the sales period. If one firm uses the derogatory ads but the other doesn't, the firm that does makes $2 million in profit and the competitor loses $2 million (as a result of a change in market share). If both firms advertise negative information about the other, then total sales of liquid dishwasher detergent will fall and both firms will lose $1 million. It's impossible for you to discuss this with the other firm. Do you run the negative ads or not?

The possible outcomes are summarized in the following table:

		A	
		Don't Advertise.	Advertise.
B	Don't Advertise.	A: $1 million profit B: $1 million profit	A: $2 million profit B: ($2 million loss)
	Advertise.	A: ($2 million loss) B: $2 million profit	A: ($1 million loss) B: ($1 million loss)

If your competitor doesn't advertise, you will get $1 million if you don't advertise either (that is, if you *cooperate*) and $2 million if you do advertise (that is, if you *defect*). If your competitor advertises (*defects*), you will *lose* $2 million if you don't advertise (*cooperate*) and $1 million if you do. No matter what the other company does, you are better off advertising. Thus, each party in this dilemma has a "dominating" strategy to defect by running the negative ads;[3] however, if both parties advertise, they both do worse than if neither advertised. It would be fairly easy to negotiate a no-advertising agreement if the parties were allowed to talk to each other, but this option isn't available.

This is a version of the classic *Prisoner's Dilemma:*

> Imagine that two accomplices in a crime have been
> apprehended by the police and are being interrogated
> separately. The police are confident that even if neither
> prisoner confesses or squeals on the other, they can convict
> both prisoners on minor charges and put them in prison for
> two years. However, the police really want at least one
> conviction on a higher charge and have offered each prisoner
> a deal. If either gives evidence that would lead to the
> conviction of his/her accomplice on higher charges, charges
> will be dropped and s/he will go free while the accomplice
> gets a ten-year sentence. If both squeal, then they will each
> get six-year sentences. Thus, for each prisoner, if his/her
> partner squeals, s/he could end up with the ten-year sentence
> while the partner goes free. What should the prisoners do?
> What would you do?[4]

The two prisoners are confronted with a situation in which they are both better off collectively if they stay silent (cooperate) than if they both squeal (defect); however, individually, each one is better off defecting, regardless of what the other party does.

A dilemma arises whenever each party in a competitive environment has a dominating strategy, but it's in the group's best interests not to choose that strategy.[5] These situations are typically referred to as *prisoner's dilemmas* (named after the story above) when there are two parties, and *social dilemmas* when they involve more than two parties. They have no easy cooperative solution. Simple analysis suggests that it is rational to defect.

While the advertising problem is a simple, one-shot decision, the commons dilemma and most managerial decisions are on-going, with repeated opportunities to cooperate or defect. In the most fundamental form of these multiple-round dilemmas, each side communicates with the other through its behavior, indicating a cooperative or competitive orientation by its choices. The multiple rounds create some incentive for the parties to cooperate in the long run as they must consider the ramifications of their actions for the future, i.e., how can they build a successful long-term competitive strategy?

Robert Axelrod has studied the prisoner's dilemma game in a multiple-round format to examine how cooperation emerges in ongoing dilemmas.[6] In his study, he invited experts to submit programs for a Computerized Prisoner's Dilemma Tournament. Each expert's entry outlined a strategy that designated each round's choices based on the history of past interactions. The object was to score as well as possible over the series of interactions. Fourteen entries and one random strategy competed against each other in the tournament.

The winner was the simplest of all the programs submitted, TIT FOR TAT. TIT FOR TAT's strategy starts first by cooperating and, thereafter, imitating the other player's previous move. Thus, as the dishwashing detergent product manager, you don't advertise the negative information about the competitor in the first round. In the next round, you do whatever your competitor did in the first round—you don't advertise if the competitor didn't, but do advertise if they did.

Axelrod published the results of the tournament and solicited entries for a second round. This time he received sixty-two entries, including many attempts to improve on TIT FOR TAT. But TIT FOR TAT won again! Why? Because it develops far more cooperative relationships than any other strategy, winning the tournament by facilitating more mutually advantageous outcomes. It creates an "integrative agreement" with as many opponents as possible.

The reasons for TIT FOR TAT's success are explained in the following prescriptions that Axelrod offers for people facing ongoing dilemmas.

Prescription 1: Don't be envious.

People tend to use as a standard of comparison their own success relative to others. This standard leads to envy—and in social dilemmas, envy is self-destructive. A better standard of comparison is how well you are doing relative to how well someone else could be doing in your place. Given the other side's strategies, are you doing as well as possible?

TIT FOR TAT won the tournament because it did well when played against a wide variety of other strategies; however, TIT FOR TAT never once scored better in a game than the other player! It can't. TIT FOR TAT achieves either the same score as the other player, or a little less.

The moral here is that there is no point in being envious of the other person's success because, in long-term relationships, you need the other person's success to do well yourself. Remember the object of the game: to score as well as possible over a series of interactions with another player who is also trying to score well. This says nothing about scoring better than your opponent on any particular round.

Prescription 2: Don't be the first to defect.

Avoid unnecessary conflict by cooperating as long as the other side does—be nice. However, a couple of important qualifications are necessary here. First, if the long-term relationship between the two parties isn't important relative to the immediate gains available from not cooperating, or defecting, then simply waiting for the other to defect is not a good idea. If you're not likely to see the other person again, defecting right away is more profitable than being nice. Second, if everyone else is using a strategy of always defecting, then you can do no better than to use this same strategy.

Prescription 3: Reciprocate both cooperation and defection.

TIT FOR TAT represents a balance between retaliation and forgiveness. If you punish the other side for defecting by getting back at them for more than their one defection, you risk escalation. On the other hand, if you don't retaliate in some way for their defection, you risk being exploited. The most effective level of retaliation and forgiveness depends on the situation. In particular, if you are risking unending mutual retaliation, then a generous level of forgiveness is best. But, if your strategy makes you an easy target for exploitation, then an excess of forgiveness is costly.

Prescription 4: Don't be too clever.

Your strategy needs to be clear if you want the other side to understand your message. Keeping your intentions hidden is useful in a fixed-pie situation, where your benefit comes at the expense of the other party's, but otherwise it doesn't always pay to be so clever. In the prisoner's dilemma, you benefit from the other side's cooperation. The trick is to encourage that cooperation. A good way to do so is to make it clear that you will reciprocate any cooperation and any defection. Words can help, but actions speak louder. That is why TIT FOR TAT is so effective.

TIT FOR TAT is such a successful strategy because it is nice, retaliatory, forgiving, and clear. Its niceness prevents you from getting into unnecessary trouble. Its retaliation discourages the other side from persisting in any defection. Its forgiveness helps restore mutual cooperation. And its clarity makes your strategy understandable to the other side, thereby eliciting long-term cooperation.

The foundation of this cooperation is not really trust, but the durability of the relationship. There is a difference between trusting someone and having a tangible incentive to maintain the relationship. Thus, whether the parties trust each other is less important in the long-run than whether the conditions are ripe for building a stable pattern of cooperation.

MORE THAN TWO PARTIES—SOCIAL DILEMMAS

The logic of this advice for two-party negotiations also applies when more than two parties are involved in the dilemma. Price wars, advertising wars, and military competition can all be positively influenced using the above insights. Consider the following scenarios:

The Budget Dilemma. It is the end of the fiscal year in your organization. About 20 percent of this year's budget remains unspent. As with most organizations, next year's budget is based on your use of this year's budget. Thus, the more resources your group uses now, the more you are likely to be allocated in future budgets. So, what do you do? Do you go on a spending spree, making sure that you spend all of this year's allocation (and maybe even a little more), or do you end the fiscal year with money to spare?

Southern California Drought. You live in Santa Barbara, an oceanside community that has been experiencing a drought for the past five years.[7] The rainfall expected for this year will not alleviate the drought conditions. The city has been under voluntary water conservation measures. These measures strongly discourage watering lawns and gardens, washing cars, and any other nonessential use of water. Your house has an interior courtyard garden that is not visible from the street. It was one of the major reasons you bought this house and you have filled the garden with many expensive plants. No one could tell if you were watering it. What would you do: water your garden or follow the voluntary water conservation guidelines?

Public Television. If you watch and enjoy public television, you are asked to contribute money in support of it. In fact, you are generally asked to contribute less than the value you place on the programming you watch—thus, your contributions are probably a good economic value. However, your individual contribution isn't likely to be enough to determine whether a program remains on the air; you are really dependent for that outcome on the contributions of others. If you don't contribute, you're better off economically because you get to watch the programs for free. So, do you contribute to public television?

Ordering Lunch. You're having lunch with six business acquaintances. The waiter taking your orders informs you that it's the restaurant's policy to have one check per table. You could either order an inexpensive salad or a moderately expensive steak. What factors enter into your decision about what to order?

What's common in each of these situations is that rational behavior for the individual is clearly not rational behavior for the group. In the budget dilemma, the organization as a whole is clearly better off if each department uses only those fiscal resources it actually needs. However, each department's incentive is to use as much as possible, regardless of its need. The same is true for you as the homeowner in southern California. No one will know if you don't abide by the voluntary water conservation measures, and you'll be able to enjoy the continued beauty of your interior courtyard; however, the community's water will quickly be used up if everyone behaves this way. The same reasoning holds true for contributions to public television. If every viewer chose the strategy that made him or her personally better off—not contributing while continuing to enjoy the benefits of public television— public television would cease to exist and viewers would lose a valuable "good."

At the luncheon, if you expect the group to split the check equally, then you may be tempted into ordering a more expensive meal. After all, ordering the salad instead of the steak saves $6 for the group but only $1 for you. Why subsidize the others' meals by ordering an inexpensive entree and splitting the cost of all six equally. If this analysis sounds offensive, why is the average restaurant bill higher when only one check is allowed per table than when individual bills are issued? There is clearly little incentive for frugality unless each person is issued a separate check based on what he or she ordered.[8]

With more than two parties, the prisoner's dilemma becomes a social dilemma and it gets harder to create cooperation among the parties. Since more people are involved, the negative effect of a defection is spread out and has less impact on any one person. In addition, as the number of people increases, the anonymity of a defection also increases; nobody will know you didn't contribute to public television.[9] As a result, more defections can be expected as the number of people involved in the dilemma increases.

Despite this logic, the level of cooperation in many social dilemma contexts is high. Why? One reason is that many people believe cooperating is the right thing to do.[10] Cooperation is even greater if you have the chance to talk with others about the dilemma.[11]

It's easy to see that simple answers don't exist for most competitive problems. Far too often a very simple strategy escalates a conflict because the parties don't stop to consider the opponent's response. You'll always find people who would rather defect than cooperate; nevertheless, the strategies we've discussed can improve your chance of getting cooperation in solving dilemmas.

THE FREQUENT-FLIER PROGRAMS REVISITED

In Chapter 1, we discussed briefly the story of frequent-flier programs. Now we know to categorize these programs as a social dilemma. Each airline had the incentive to promote its own service; however, collectively, all airlines were worse off as a result. Instead of solving this social dilemma, the airlines escalated the conflict. Reconsider this example now that you have more insight on how the frequent-flier mess could have been negotiated rationally.

A central theme of this book is that managers in a negotiation often fail to act rationally because of common mental errors or biases, and that you need to monitor your own decisions for these biases and anticipate them in your competitors' decisions. These common biases were critical in creating the $12 billion debt that the airlines face. A simple assessment is that it was an escalatory spiral that got out of hand. Every airline tried to offer the best possible program, but as they continued to improve the quality, the costs of the programs grew substantially beyond their value. The airlines were asking the wrong question. They were asking how they could gain market share, when they should have asked how they could increase their profitability.

Another crucial bias was the airlines' failure to consider the decisions of their competitors. Delta offered triple miles on December 15, 1987. We argue that if Delta had simply considered the likely responses of their competitors, Delta would have realized the other airlines would meet or beat their triple mileage offer. Without thinking about competitors, it's easy to see how the marketing department at Delta could argue that triple mileage would bring them customers. Instead, everyone else matched the offer, and Delta and the other airlines suffered huge financial losses.

Are we placing all of the blame on Delta? Certainly not! All of the major carriers were to blame. They failed to think about

Delta's decision in advance of the triple mileage announcement. They could have remembered the auto industry rebate wars and modeled their behavior on Iacocca's actions, but none of them did. If one of the airlines had announced to the press that it was scaling back its program, but that it would meet or beat any promotion offered, it would have eliminated Delta's incentive to announce the triple mileage offer; however, all of the airlines were too busy thinking about their own decisions, and not thinking about the decisions of their competitors.

We have spoken to a number of airline executives involved in the triple mileage programs. What's amazing about these discussions is that the executives go to great lengths to explain how wonderful it is to have the loyal customers created by the frequent-flier programs. They fail to acknowledge that customer loyalty to other airlines creates a real problem for them. Nor do they emphasize the huge debt. Rather, the executives try to justify their failed course of action. Why? They are biased against seeing the entire campaign as a multibillion dollar mistake created by a series of irrational decisions; this keeps them from having to admit the error and prevents them from learning from the past and formulating a rational strategy for the future.

The airlines failed to identify the true objective of their shareholders—to make money. They erroneously defined the problem as the need to beat the other airlines. Unfortunately, they all beat each other, while the passengers collected billions of dollars in free trips. The airlines didn't realize that, with the relatively fixed number of air passengers, any promotion that's simply matched by competitors only benefits the customer. No airline wins. American Airlines should have thought more about this matching behavior when they created their program, Delta should have thought it through before announcing triple miles, and all airlines should have considered how to manage the decisions of the other parties involved.

CONCLUSIONS

Many of the strategies for managing social dilemmas that we've described throughout this chapter could have helped the airlines.

Without actually discussing its competitive problems, each airline could have taken cooperative actions that would have benefited them all. If they had mutually reduced or eliminated their frequent-flier programs, they all could have found an integrative, mutually beneficial agreement. For now, however, customers continue to fly free—courtesy of the airlines' irrationality.

CHAPTER
18

Conclusion
Negotiating Rationally in an Irrational World

We've given you a basic framework for negotiating rationally. Just reading about the mistakes to avoid and examining the structure for negotiating rationally has already made you a better negotiator. And while we'd like to close with a set of easy rules that will work in all your future negotiations, you've learned in this book that negotiation is too complex for such a simple conclusion. Each negotiation requires careful evaluation based on its own characteristics. And, of course, each negotiation must be analyzed rationally.

One of the surest ways to negotiate more rationally is to be well prepared. There are questions you can ask before a negotiation to help you think it through in a careful and systematic way and reduce the impact of any biases on your judgment. In addition, careful preparation can point out where you are missing information that you should collect in the negotiation process. Being well prepared can also help you distinguish good agreements from poor agreements and better anticipate what might unfold in the negotiation, so you can be ready to respond rationally.

While initially you have to prepare before you see how your opponent will behave, it doesn't mean you should ignore the other party, or their influence on the negotiation, as you prepare. Predicting your opponents' reaction to your proposals is a critical component of negotiating rationally. Of course, you might hope to be facing someone who has also read *Negotiating Rationally* and is working to reach the best possible agreements. But what if you're not so lucky? What if you must negotiate with the opponent from hell—an irrational, distributive, antagonistic negotiator? Will the advice in this book work? The answer is "yes." Again, while our advice won't guarantee your success, it gives you the best chance to maximize your outcomes—when facing any opponent.

Many of the biggest mistakes in negotiation result not from answering questions incorrectly, but from never asking the right ones. The questions you should ask also summarize the key issues presented in this book.

QUESTIONS FOR AVOIDING COMMON MISTAKES IN NEGOTIATION

You must carefully analyze and evaluate your decision processes to reduce the effects of any biases. To do so ask yourself the following seven questions.

- Are you pursuing a negotiated course of action only to justify an earlier decision?
- Are you assuming that what's good for you is necessarily bad for your opponent, and vice-versa?
- Are you being irrationally affected by an initial anchor price?
- Is there another frame that would put a different perspective on the negotiation?
- Are you being affected by readily available information, and ignoring other valid, but less accessible data?
- Have you fully thought about the decisions of your opponent?
- Are you placing too much confidence in your own fallible judgment?

By auditing your decisions for these errors, you greatly improve your chances of not falling victim to these biases.

It's also just as critical to anticipate the decisions and behaviors of the other party. Thus, you should ask the same seven questions about your predictions for your opponent's behavior. Irrational opponents are more likely to escalate conflict, assume a mythical fixed-pie, stick to their anchor, have a limited frame, use only limited information, ignore your perspective, and be overconfident in the negotiation. If you realize in advance the high likelihood of finding these biases, you can better anticipate how to counteract the other party's irrationality. You can also decide when you would be better off walking away instead of accepting an agreement based on the irrational demands of your opponent. Remember, it's not always rational to get to "yes."

QUESTIONS FOR STRUCTURING A RATIONAL NEGOTIATION

Don't forget the critical steps for thinking rationally in negotiation. The three most important steps suggest good questions to ask yourself before every negotiation.

1. What is your reservation price?

Before any negotiation begins, think about your BATNA to establish your reservation price. In addition, always think how you can improve your reservation price by developing your options in advance of the negotiation.

2. What are your interests?

You must recognize the interests underlying your positions, have the best possible understanding of those interests, and be as inclusive as you can in identifying them.

3. Comparatively, how important is each negotiation issue to you?

Only by knowing the relative importance of the issues can you think systematically about making trade-offs that create joint gain.
    It's also important to ask these questions when thinking about your opponents. Whether they're rational or irrational, you need to think about their reservation price(s), interests, and the com-

parative importance of the issues to them. The answers to these questions will tell you what information you need about your opponent. Knowing their reservation price is necessary for you to identify the bargaining zone in order to analyze the distributive dimension of the negotiation. Thinking about the interests and comparative importance of issues to the other side also helps you identify optimal trade-offs.

What if your opponents are threatening you with impasse? What if they're making unreasonable demands? Executives often face such barriers in negotiation. Many respond by making a quick intuitive judgment—they either give in to the irrational opponent or walk away from the negotiation. By negotiating rationally, however, you will be able to understand your opponent well enough to devise the strategy that will maximize your interests in the situation.

CAUCUSING AND THE AGREEMENT PROCESS

You enter a negotiation well prepared. You are ready to negotiate rationally. The negotiation begins. Your preparation is over, right? Wrong! The negotiation process itself provides you with a wealth of information to update your rational negotiation strategy. Don't simply escalate commitment to your initial strategy. Instead, use each break in the negotiation as an opportunity to reassess, incorporate new information, and reformulate your strategy.

A common negotiation tactic is to put the opponent on the spot, and use their reflexive, ill-developed responses against them. You can defend against this tactic by taking a break or caucusing with your negotiation group when your next move isn't rationally developed yet. It's better to take time out or call a caucus than to blurt out a position that may be used against you for the rest of the negotiation.

Because your negotiation preparation includes updating and reassessing your information, even during the negotiation or during caucuses, it's critical to realize what you don't know going in and use the negotiation process as an opportunity to fill in the gaps. Did you learn anything in the recent interaction that changes your assessment of your opponent's reservation price or interests, or the relative importance he or she attaches to various issues?

What is your updated assessment of the bargaining zone? Where should you now look for trades? Constant reassessment is essential to rational negotiation.

Once you reach agreement, you should evaluate that agreement and look for post-settlement settlements. Is it possible that there's a better agreement available for both parties? Is it possible to obtain a better price? Would it have been worth the risk to hold out for a better price? The answers to these questions may allow you to change the agreement or, at a minimum, teach you something useful for future negotiations.

FINAL COMMENTS

It's strange to close a book with questions rather than answers. Yet, it's appropriate here because there are no simple answers, only a set of questions to guide you in a rational negotiation process. You will dramatically increase your overall effectiveness as a negotiator if you can do the following:

- Audit your own decision processes
- Actively consider the decision processes of your opponent
- Make your best assessment of reservation prices, interests, and the comparative importance of issues
- View the negotiation process as an opportunity to collect and update your information.

So, will you now reach a great agreement in every negotiation? Will you be able to totally disarm irrational negotiators and make them sane? Probably not! But you've known that since the first chapter. What you will do is increase your odds of getting good outcomes—by negotiating rationally.

No simple set of rules will work in every case. Any book that offers such a guarantee is suffering the bias of overconfidence. But armed with our guide, you can be confident that you know how to negotiate rationally. We do guarantee that you've improved your chances of doing as well as you can—so get out there and negotiate!

Notes

CHAPTER 1. Introduction to Rational Thinking in Negotiation

1. R. Fisher and W. Ury, *Getting to yes* (Boston: Houghton-Mifflin, 1981).
2. A. Zipser, Sky's the limit? Frequent-flier programs are ballooning out of control, *Barron's*, 17 September 1990, pp. 16–17, *44,* estimates the number of miles accumulated at 800 billion. 20,000 miles are typically redeemable for a free flight within the continental United States. If we value a free flight anywhere in the U.S. at $300, the estimated debt of the airlines can be approximated at $12 billion.
3. Free-for-all in the skies, *Time,* 7 March, 1988, p. 50.
4. Cutting back on flier's freebies, *Fortune,* 6 June 1988, pp. 149–52.

CHAPTER 2. The Irrational Escalation of Commitment

1. Suitors for Federated Department Stores show few signs of weakening resolve in bidding war, *The Wall Street Journal,* 25 March 1988, p. 4.
2. Is anyone minding Federated's store as battle rages to take over retailer? *The Wall Street Journal,* 25 March 1988, p. 4.
3. H. Lampert, Citizen Campeau, *Business Month,* October 1988, p. 42.
4. A. Rapaport, *Creating shareholder value* (New York: Free Press, 1986).
5. T. Tyler and R. Hastie, The social consequences of cognitive illusions, in M. H. Bazerman, R. J. Lewicki, and B. Sheppard, eds., *Handbook of negotiation research: Research on negotiation in organizations,* vol. 3 (Greenwich, Conn.: JAI Press, 1991).

6. M. H. Bazerman, T. Giuliano, and A. Appleman, Escalation in individual and group decision making, *Organizational Behavior and Human Decision Processes* 33 (1984), 141–52; J. Brockner and J. Rubin, *The social psychology of entrapment in escalating conflict* (New York: Springer-Verlag, 1985); B. M. Staw, Knee deep in the big muddy: A study of escalating commitment to a chosen course of action, *Organizational Behavior and Human Performance* 16 (1976), 27–44; B. M. Staw, The escalation of commitment to a course of action, *Academy of Management Review* 6 (1981), 577–87; A. Teger *Too much invested to quit: The psychology of the escalation of conflict* (New York: Pergamon Press, 1980).

7. M. H. Bazerman, R. Beekun, and F. Schoorman, Performance evaluation in a dynamic context: The impact of a prior commitment to the ratee, *Journal of Applied Psychology* 67 (1982), 873–76; F. Schoorman, Escalation bias in performance appraisals: An unintended consequence of supervisor participation in hiring decisions, *Journal of Applied Psychology* 73 (1988), 58–62.

8. M. Shubik, The dollar auction game: A paradox in noncooperative behavior and escalation, *Journal of Conflict Resolution* 15 (1971), 109–11.

9. Teger, *Too much invested to quit.*

10. B. M. Staw and J. Ross, Commitment in an experimenting society: An experiment on the attribution of leadership from administrative scenarios, *Journal of Applied Psychology* 65 (1980), 249–60.

11. Staw, *The escalation of commitment.*

12. T. Peters and R. Waterman, *In search of excellence: Lessons from America's best-run companies* (New York: Harper & Row, 1982).

CHAPTER 3. The Mythical Fixed-Pie

1. J. Adams, *Conceptual blockbusting* (San Francisco: San Francisco Book Co., 1979); M. H. Bazerman, *Judgment in managerial decision making,* 2d ed. (New York: John Wiley and Sons, 1990); W. Winklegren, *How to solve problems* (San Francisco: Freeman, 1974).

2. The problem has been used without original reference by many previous authors.

3. We are indebted to C. Stillinger, M. Epelbaum, D. Keltner, and L. Ross, *The 'reactive devaluation' barrier to conflict resolution,* working paper, Stanford University, 1990, for this fascinating quotation.

4. A. Bernstein, *Grounded: Frank Lorenzo and the destruction of Eastern Airlines* (New York: Simon & Schuster, 1990).

5. Ibid., p. 41.

6. The game of chicken is played by two drivers, who drive their trucks toward each other on a one-lane road, each hoping that the other will "chicken" out and veer off first. You win when the other driver chickens out before you. If neither driver chickens out, both lose big.

7. L. Thompson, Information exchange in negotiation, *Journal of Experimental Social Psychology* 27 (1991), 161–79.

8. Ibid; M. A. Neale and M. H. Bazerman, The effects of framing and negotiator overconfidence on bargainer behavior, *Academy of Management Journal* 28 (1985), 34–49.

9. S. Oskamp, Attitudes towards U.S. and Russian actions: A double standard, *Psychological Reports* 16 (1965), 43–46; Stillinger, Epelbaum, Keltner, and Ross, The 'reactive devaluation' barrier to conflict resolution.

CHAPTER 4. Anchoring and Adjustment

1. Bernstein, *Grounded,* p. 207.

2. Ibid.

3. E. E. Joyce and G. C. Biddle, Anchoring and adjustment in probabilistic inference in auditing, *Journal of Accounting Research* 19 (Spring 1981), 123.

4. G. B. Northcraft and M. A. Neale, Amateurs, experts, and real estate: An anchoring-and-adjustment perspective on property pricing decisions, *Organizational Behavior and Human Decision Processes* 39 (1987), 84–97.

5. R. M. Liebert, W. P. Smith, J. H. Hill, and M. Keiffer, The effects of information and magnitude of initial offer on interpersonal negotiation, *Journal of Experimental Social Psychology,* 4 (1968), 431–41; G. A. Yukl, Effects of situational variables and opponent concessions on a bargainer's perceptions, aspirations, and concessions, *Journal of Personality and Social Psychology* 29 (1974), 227–36.

6. E. A. Locke and G. P. Latham, *Goal setting: A motivational technique that really works!* (Englewood Cliffs, N.J.: Prentice-Hall, 1990).

7. M. A. Neale and M. H. Bazerman, The effect of externally set goals on reaching integrative agreements in competitive markets, *Journal of Occupational Behavior* 6 (1985), 19–32; M. H. Bazerman, T. Magliozzi, and M. A. Neale, Integrative bargaining in a competitive market, *Organizational Behavior and Human Performance* 35 (1985), 294–313; V. L. Huber and M. A. Neale, Effects of cognitive heuristics and goals on negotiator performance and subsequent goal

setting, *Organizational Behavior and Human Decision Processes* 38 (1986), 342–64; V. L. Huber and M. A. Neale, Effects of self and competitor goals on performance in an interdependent bargaining task, *Journal of Applied Psychology* 72 (1987), 197–203.

8. Huber and Neale, Effects of self and competitor goals on performance.

CHAPTER 5. Framing Negotiations

1. Adapted from J. E. Russo and P. J. Schoemaker, *Decision traps* (New York: Doubleday, 1989).

2. R. Thaler, Using mental accounting in a theory of purchasing behavior, *Marketing Science* 4 (1985), 12–13.

3. A. Tversky and D. Kahneman, The framing of decisions and the psychology of choice, *Science* 40 (1981), 453–63.

4. P. Slovic, B. Fischhoff, and S. Lichtenstein, Facts versus fears: Understanding perceived risk, in D. Kahneman, P. Slovic, and A. Tversky, eds., *Judgment under uncertainty: Heuristics and biases* (New York: Cambridge University Press, 1982).

5. P. Slovic, Information processing, situation specificity, and the generality of risk taking behavior, *Journal of Personality and Social Psychology* 22 (1972), 128–34.

6. D. Kahneman and A. Tversky, Prospect theory: An analysis of decision under risk, *Econometrica* 47 (1979), 263–91.

7. D. Kahneman, J. L. Knetsch, and R. Thaler, Experimental tests of the endowment effect and Coase theorem, *Journal of Political Economy,* in press.

8. The coffee mugs were valued at approximately $5.00 each.

9. The "deal" purportedly offered to President Hussein has never been made public; however, to reconstruct it, we drew from a number of sources including: *The Wall Street Journal,* 10 August 1990, p. 3; *Time,* 20 August 1990, pp. 27–28; *The New York Times,* 5 August 1990, pp. 1, 14–15; and Roger Fisher, "Getting to 'Yes' with Saddam: How words can win," *The Washington Post,* sec. K, Commentary and Opinion.

10. Neale and Bazerman, The effects of framing and negotiator overconfidence.

11. M. H. Bazerman, T. Magliozzi, and M. A. Neale, The acquisition of an integrative response in a competitive market simulation, *Organizational Behavior and Human Performance* 34 (1985), 294–313.

12. See, for example, Bazerman, Magliozzi, and Neale, The acquisition

of an integrative response; Neale and Bazerman, The effects of framing and negotiator overconfidence; or M. A. Neale and G. B. Northcraft, Experts, amateurs, and refrigerators: Comparing expert and amateur decision making on a novel task, *Organizational Behavior and Human Decision Processes* 38 (1986), 305–17; M. A. Neale, V. L. Huber, and G. B. Northcraft, The framing of negotiations: Context versus task frames, *Organizational Behavior and Human Decision Processes* 39 (1987), 228–41.

13. Bazerman, Magliozzi, and Neale, Integrative bargaining; Neale, Huber, and Northcraft, The framing of negotiations.

CHAPTER 6. Availability of Information

1. Most scientists believe that a catastrophic New Madrid earthquake (a magnitude of 8.0 or greater on the Richter scale) will occur on the New Madrid fault sometime during the next 500 to 1500 years.

2. A. Tversky and D. Kahneman, Judgment under uncertainty: Heuristics and biases, *Science* 185 (1974), 1124–31.

3. M. G. Wilson, G. B. Northcraft, and M. A. Neale, Information competition and vividness effect in on-line judgments, *Organizational Behavior and Human Decision Processes* 44 (1989), 132–39.

4. Tversky and Kahneman, Judgment under uncertainty.

5. M. A. Neale, The effects of negotiation and arbitration cost salience on bargainer behavior: The role of arbitrator and constituency on negotiator judgments, *Organizational Behavior and Human Performance* 34 (1984), 97–111.

6. Insure against future repairs? *Consumer Reports,* April 1990, pp. 226–27.

CHAPTER 7. The Winner's Curse

1. W. Samuelson and M.H. Bazerman, The winner's curse in bilateral negotiations, in V. Smith, ed., *Research in Experimental Economics,* vol. 3, pp. 105–37 (Greenwich, Conn.: JAI Press, 1985).

2. G. Akerlof, The market for lemons: Quality uncertainty and the market mechanism, *Quarterly Journal of Economics* 84 (1970), 488–500.

3. M. H. Bazerman and J. S. Carroll, Negotiator cognition, in B. M. Staw and L. L. Cummings, eds., *Research in organizational behavior,* vol. 9, pp. 247–88 (Greenwich, Conn.: JAI Press, 1987).

4. Akerlof, The market for lemons.

5. S. Ball, Experimental evidence on the bilateral winner's curse, Ph.D. diss., Northwestern University, 1991.

6. M. A. Neale and M. H. Bazerman, The role of perspective-taking ability in negotiating under different forms of arbitration, *Industrial and Labor Relations Review* 36 (1983), 378–88.

7. M. H. Bazerman and M. A. Neale, Heuristics in negotiation: Limitations to dispute resolution effectiveness, in M. H. Bazerman and R. J. Lewicki, eds., *Negotiating in organizations* (Beverly Hills, Calif.: Sage, 1983).

8. Ball, Experimental evidence on the bilateral winner's curse.

9. D. Pruitt, *Negotiation behavior* (New York: Academic Press, 1981).

CHAPTER 8. Overconfidence and Negotiation Behavior

1. B. Fischhoff, P. Slovic, and S. Lichtenstein, Knowing with certainty: The appropriateness of extreme confidence, *Journal of Experimental Psychology: Human Perception and Performance* 3 (1977), 552–64; A. Koriat, S. Lichtenstein, and B. Fischhoff, Reasons for confidence, *Journal of Experimental Psychology: Human Learning and Memory* 6 (1980), 107–18; S. Lichtenstein and B. Fischhoff, Do those who know more also know more about how much they know? The calibration of probability judgments, *Organizational Behavior and Human Performance* 20 (1977), 159–83; S. Lichtenstein and B. Fischhoff, Training for calibration, *Organizational Behavior and Human Performance* 26 (1980), 149–71.

2. A more realistic figure, based upon the company's financial position was closer to $100/share (How Ross Johnson blew the deal, *Fortune,* 24 April 1989).

3. Neale and Bazerman, The effect of perspective-taking ability under alternative forms of arbitration.

4. M. H. Bazerman and M. A. Neale, Improving effectiveness under final offer arbitration: The role of selection and training, *Journal of Applied Psychology* 67 (1982), 543–48.

5. S. Lichtenstein, B. Fischhoff, and L. D. Phillips, Calibration of probabilities: State of the art to 1980, in D. Kahneman, P. Slovic, and A. Tversky, eds., *Judgment under uncertainty: Heuristics and biases* (New York: Cambridge University Press, 1982).

6. Tversky and Kahneman, Judgment under uncertainty.

7. S. E. Taylor and J. D. Brown, Illusion and well-being: A social psychological perspective, *Psychological Bulletin,* 103 (1988), 193–210; Tyler and Hastie, The social consequences of cognitive illusions;

R. E. Nisbett and L. Ross, *Human inference: Strategies and short-comings of social judgment* (Englewood Cliffs, N.J.: Prentice-Hall, 1980).

8. Taylor and Brown, Illusion and well-being.

9. B. R. Schlenker and R. S. Miller, Egocentrism in groups: Self-serving biases or logical information processing? *Journal of Personality and Social Psychology* 35 (1977), 755–64; S. E. Taylor and J. H. Koivumaki, The perception of self and others: Acquaintanceship, affect, and actor-observer differences, *Journal of Personality and Social Psychology* 33 (1976), 403–8; Nisbett and Ross, *Human inference.*

10. R. M. Kramer, E. Newton, and P. Pommerenke, Self-enhancement bias and negotiator judgment: Effects of self-esteem and mood, working paper, Graduate School of Business, Stanford University, 1991.

11. E. Langer, The illusion of control, *Journal of Personality and Social Psychology* 32 (1975), 311–28; E. Langer and J. Roth, Heads I win, tails, it's chance. The illusion of control as a function of the sequence of outcomes in a purely chance task, *Journal of Personality and Social Psychology* 32 (1975), 951–55; J. Crocker, Biased questions in judgment of covariation studies, *Personality and Social Psychology Bulletin* 8 (1982), 214–20.

12. Adapted from a series of studies conducted by P. Wason in the 1960s.

13. C. G. Lord, L. Ross, and M. R. Lepper, Biased assimilation and attitude polarization: The effects of prior theories on subsequently considered evidence, *Journal of Personality and Social Psychology* 37 (1979), 2098–2109.

CHAPTER 9. Thinking Rationally about Negotiation

1. J. Sebenius, International negotiation: Problems and new approaches, working paper, Kennedy School of Government, Harvard University, 1989.

2. D. Lax and J. Sebenius, *The manager as negotiator* (New York: Free Press, 1986).

3. Fisher and Ury, *Getting to yes.*

4. Ibid.

5. D. Pruitt and J. Rubin, *Social Conflict* (New York: Random House, 1986).

6. Lax and Sebenius, *The manager as negotiator.*

7. R. E. Walton and R. B. McKersie, *A behavioral theory of labor negotiation* (New York: McGraw-Hill, 1965).
8. H. Raiffa, *The art and science of negotiation* (Cambridge, Mass.: Belknap, 1982).
9. M. Follett, Constructive Conflict, in E. Fox and L. Urwick, eds., *Dynamic Administration: The Collected Papers of Mary Parker Follett* (New York: Hippocrene, 1982).

CHAPTER 10. Negotiations in a Joint Venture

1. For simplicity, all numbers used in this case will reflect net profit before taxes in current dollars. Both companies are assumed to attempt to maximize their expected value. In this chapter we will not deal with issues such as the trade-off between dollars and a share of profitability.
2. D. Pruitt, Achieving integrative agreements, in M. H. Bazerman and R. J. Lewicki, eds., *Negotiating in organizations* (Beverly Hills, CA: Sage, 1983).

CHAPTER 11. Rational Strategies for Creating Integrative Agreements

1. L. Thompson, Negotiation: Empirical evidence and theoretical issues, *Psychological Bulletin* 108 (1990), 515–32; R. Lewicki and J. Litterer, *Negotiation* (Homewood, Ill.: R. D. Irwin, 1985); R. E. Walton and R. B. McKersie, *A behavioral theory of labor negotiation* (New York: McGraw-Hill, 1965).
2. M. H. Bazerman, L. Russ, and E. Yakura, Post-settlement in dyadic negotiations: The need for renegotiation in complex environments, *Negotiation Journal* 3 (1987), 283–97.
3. Ibid.
4. Lax and Sebenius, *The manager as negotiator.*
5. Ibid.
6. Pruitt, Achieving integrative agreements.

CHAPTER 12. Are You an Expert?

1. L. M. Fisher, "Winery's answer to the critics: Print good and bad reviews," *The New York Times,* 9 January 1991, Media Business Section, p. 11.
2. T. Tritch and D. Lohse, The Pros flub our tax test (again), *Money,* March 1991, 96–111.

3. The store owner subsequently sued Wrzensinski, and the case was settled out of court.

4. J. Leptich, Boy sued over baseball card, *Chicago Tribune,* 10 November 1990, sec. 1, p. 1.

5. R. M. Dawes, *Rational choice in an uncertain world* (New York: Harcourt Brace Jovanovich, 1988).

6. J. H. Kagel and D. Levin, The winner's curse and public information in common value auctions, *American Economic Review* 76 (1986), p. 917.

7. A. Tversky and D. Kahneman, Rational choice and the framing of decisions, *Journal of Business* 59 (1986), 251–84.

8. S. Ball, M. H. Bazerman, and J. S. Carroll, An evaluation of learning in the bilateral winner's curse, *Organizational Behavior and Human Decision Processes* 48 (1991), 1–27.

9. A. H. Hastorf and H. Cantril, They say a game: A case study, *Journal of Abnormal and Social Psychology* 49 (1954), 129–34.

10. E. A. Mannix, G. B. Northcraft, and M. A. Neale, Integrative and distributive negotiation training and experience: A competitive advantage? working paper, Northwestern University, 1991.

11. Neale and Northcraft, Experts, amateurs, and refrigerators.

12. Northcraft and Neale, Experts, amateurs, and real estate, pp. 84–97.

13. V. L. Huber, G. B. Northcraft, and M. A. Neale, Effects of decision context and anchoring bias on employment screening decisions, *Organizational Behavior and Human Decision Processes* 40 (1990), 149–69.

CHAPTER 13. Fairness, Emotion, and Rationality in Negotiation

1. J. S. Adams, Inequity in social exchange, in L. Berkowitz ed., *Advances in experimental social psychology,* vol. 2 (New York: Academic Press, 1965); M. Deutsch, Equity, equality, and need: What determines which value will be used as the basis of distributive justice, *Journal of Social Issues* 31 (1975), 137–49; and M. Deutsch, *Distributive Justice* (New Haven: Yale University Press, 1984).

2. D. Kahneman, J. L. Knetsch, and R. Thaler, Fairness as a constraint on profit seeking: Entitlements in the market, *American Economic Review* 76 (1987), 728–41.

3. W. Guth, R. Schmittberger, and B. Schwarze, An experimental analysis of ultimatum bargaining, *Journal of Economic Behavior and Organization* 3 (1982), 367–88.

4. J. Ochs and A. E. Roth, An experimental study of sequential bargaining, *American Economic Review* 79 (1989), 335–85.

5. Reported in R. B. Cialdini, *Influence: How and why people agree to things* (New York: Morrow, 1984).

6. A. M. Isen and P. F. Levine, Effects of feeling good on helping: Cookies and kindness, *Journal of Personality and Social Psychology* 21 (1972), 384–88; C. Gouaux, Induced affective states and interpersonal attraction, *Journal of Personality and Social Psychology* 20 (1971), 37–43; R. Veitch and W. Griffitt, Good news—bad news: Affective and interpersonal effects, *Journal of Applied Social Psychology* 6 (1976), 69–75; R. A. Baron, Reducing organizational conflict: An incompatible response approach, *Journal of Applied Psychology* 69 (1984), 272–79; A. M. Isen, The influence of positive affect on cognitive organization, paper presented at the Stanford Conference on Aptitude, Learning, and Instruction: Affective and Cognitive Processes, 1983; A. M. Isen and K. A. Daubman, The influence of affect on categorization, *Journal of Personality and Social Psychology* 47 (1984), 1206–17; A. M. Isen, M. M. Johnson, E. Mertz, and G. F. Robinson, The influence of positive affect on the unusualness of work associations, *Journal of Personality and Social Psychology* 48 (1985), 1413–26.

7. A. M. Isen, T. E. Nygren, and F. G. Ashby, The influence of positive affect on the subjective utility of gains and losses, *Journal of Personality and Social Psychology* 55 (1988), 710–17; A. M. Isen and R. A. Baron, Positive affect as a factor in organizational behavior, in L. L. Cummings and B. M. Staw, eds., *Research in Organizational Behavior,* vol. 13, pp. 1–53 (Greenwich, Conn.: JAI Press, 1991).

8. P. J. Carnevale and A. M. Isen, The influence of positive affect and visual access on the discovery of integrative solutions in bilateral negotiations, *Organizational Behavior and Human Decision Processes* 37 (1986), 1–13.

9. Kramer, Newton, and Pommerenke, Self-enhancement bias and negotiator judgment.

10. S. Siegel and L. Fouraker, *Bargaining and group decision making: Experiments in bilateral monopoly* (New York: McGraw-Hill, 1960), 100.

11. H. Sondak, R. L. Pinkley, and M. A. Neale, Distributive justice in negotiations, paper presented at the Academy of Management Meetings, Miami, Fla., 1991.

12. G. Loewenstein, L. L. Thompson, and M. H. Bazerman, Social utility and decision making in interpersonal contexts, *Journal of Personality and Social Psychology* 57 (1989), 426–41.

13. Ibid.

14. M. H. Bazerman, G. Loewenstein, and S. B. White, The inconsistent role of social comparison in individual's evaluations of allocation decisions, working paper, Dispute Resolution Research Center, Northwestern University, 1991.

CHAPTER 14. Negotiating in Groups and Organizations

1. M. H. Bazerman, E. A. Mannix, and L. L. Thompson, Groups as mixed-motive negotiations, in E. J. Lawler and B. Markovshy, eds., *Advances in group processes: Theory and research,* vol. 5 (Greenwich, Conn.: JAI Press, 1988).

2. K. Auletta, *Greed and glory on Wall Street: The fall of the house of Lehman* (New York: Warner Books, 1986).

3. M. E. Shaw, *Group dynamics: The psychology of small group behavior* (New York: McGraw-Hill, 1976).

4. S. E. Asch, Effects of group pressure upon the modification and distortion of judgment, in H. Guetzkow, ed., *Groups, leadership, and men* (Pittsburgh, Pa.: Carnegie Press, 1951).

5. J. Adams, Toward an understanding of equity, *Journal of Abnormal and Social Psychology* 67 (1963), 422–36; G. Homans, *Social behavior: Its elementary forms* (New York: Harcourt and Brace, 1961); P. Singer, Rights and the market, in J. Arthur, and W. Shaw, eds., *Justice and economic distribution* (Englewood Cliffs, N.J.: Prentice-Hall, 1978).

6. Deutsch, Equity, equality, and need.

7. D. Kahneman, J. L. Knetsch, and R. Thaler, Fairness and the assumptions of economics, *Journal of Business* 56 (1986), 285–300; M. H. Bazerman, Norms of distributive justice in interest arbitration, *Industrial and Labor Relations Review* 38 (1985), 588–570.

8. S. S. Komorita, and J. Chertkoff, A bargaining theory of coalition formation, *Psychological Review* 80 (1973), 149–62.

9. K. Bettenhausen, and J. K. Murnighan, The emergence of norms in competitive decision making groups, *Administrative Science Quarterly* 30 (1985), 350–72.

10. The *Ledger* is based on a group simulation written by Kathleen Valley, Pamela Jiranek, John Lavine, and Max Bazerman.

11. A. P. Hare, *Handbook of small group research* (New York: Free Press, 1976); R. G. Niemi, and H. F. Weisberg, *Probability models of collective decision making* (Columbus, Oh.: Merrill Publishing, 1972); P. C. Fishburn, Simple voting systems and majority rule, *Behavioral Science* 19 (1974), 166–76.

12. D. L. Harnett, and L. L. Cummings, *Bargaining behavior* (Houston, Tex.: Dame Publishing, 1980).

13. R. A. Chechile, Logical foundations for a fair and rational method of voting, in W. Swap, ed., *Group decision making* (Beverly Hills, Calif.: Sage, 1984); C. R. Plott, Axiomatic social choice theory: An overview and interpretation, *American Journal of Political Science* 20 (1976), 511–96.

14. L. L. Thompson, E. A. Mannix, and M. H. Bazerman, Group negotiation: Effects of decision rule, agenda, and aspiration, *Journal of Personality and Social Psychology* 54 (1989), 86–95.

15. Bazerman, Mannix, and Thompson, Groups as mixed-motive negotiations.

16. Ibid.

17. E. A. Mannix, Organizations as resource dilemmas: The effects of power balance on coalition formation in small groups, *Organizational Behavior and Human Decision Processes* (in press).

CHAPTER 15. Negotiation through Third Parties

1. H. A. Landsberger, Interaction process analysis of professional behavior: A study of labor mediators in twelve labor-management disputes, *American Sociological Review* 51 (1955), 566–75; P. J. Carnevale, and J. Pegnetter, The selection of mediation tactics in public sector disputes, *Journal of Social Issues* 41 (1985), 65–82; T. Kochan, and T. Jick, The public sector mediation process, *Journal of Conflict Resolution* 22 (1978), 209–40; J. M. Hiltrop, and J. Z. Rubin, Effects of intervention conflict of interest on dispute resolution, *Journal of Personality and Social Psychology* 42 (1982), 665–72.

2. This is similar to the marriage counselor's facilitating the couple's dissolution of their marriage.

3. N. A. Thoennes, and J. Pearson, Predicting outcomes in divorce mediation: The influence of people and process, *Journal of Social Issues* 41 (1985), 115–26.

4. F. Elkouri and E. Elkouri, *How arbitration works* (Washington, D.C.: Bureau of National Affairs, 1981).

5. C. M. Stevens, Is compulsory arbitration compatible with bargaining? *Industrial Relations* 5 (1966), 38–50; W. W. Notz and F. M. Starke, The impact of final offer arbitration versus conventional arbitration on the aspirations and behaviors of bargainers, *Administrative Science Quarterly* 23 (1978), 189–203.

6. D. W. Grigsby and W. J. Bigoness, Effects of mediation and

alternative forms of arbitration on bargaining behavior—a laboratory study, *Journal of Applied Psychology* 67 (1982), 549–54; Notz and Starke, The impact of final offer arbitration; F. M. Starke and W. W. Notz, Pre- and post-intervention effects on conventional versus final offer arbitration, *Academy of Management Journal* 24 (1981), 832–50; Neale and Bazerman, The role of perspective-taking ability in negotiating under different forms of arbitration, *Industrial and Labor Relations Review,* 36 (1990) 378–88. H. S. Farber, M. A. Neale, and M. H. Bazerman, The impact of risk aversion and arbitration costs on disputed outcomes, *Industrial Relations,* 1990, 29, 361–384; T. Kochan, M. Mironi, R. Ehrenberg, J. Baderschneider, and T. Jick, *Dispute resolution under factfinding and arbitration: An empirical analysis* (New York: American Arbitration Association, 1979); J. Delaney and P. J. Feuille, Police interest arbitration: Awards and issues, *Arbitration Journal* 39 (1984), 14–24.

7. Farber, Neale, and Bazerman; Neale, The effect of negotiation and arbitration cost salience on bargainer behavior; Neale and Bazerman, The role of perspective-taking ability in negotiating under different forms of arbitration.

8. S. Zucker, Players need agents to look out for their best interests, *The Atlanta Constitution,* 28 May 1989, p. D-6.

9. B. Selcraig, The deal that went sour: Sports agents Norby Walters and Lloyd Bloom were indicted for racketeering and extortion, *Sports Illustrated,* 5 September 1988, pp. 32–3.

10. K. J. Arrow, *Applied economics* (Cambridge, Mass.: Belknap Press, 1985).

11. M. H. Bazerman, M. A. Neale, K. Valley, Y. M. Kim, and E. Zajac, The impact of agents and mediators on negotiatior behavior, *Organization Behavior and Human Decision Processes* (in press).

12. K. L. Valley, S. B. White, M. A. Neale, and M. H. Bazerman, The effect of agent's knowledge on negotiator performance in simulated real estate negotiations, *Organization Behavior and Human Decision Processes* (in press)

13. R. J. Lewicki and B. H. Sheppard, Choosing to intervene: Factors affecting the use of process and outcome control in third party dispute resolution, *Journal of Occupational Behavior* 6 (1985), 49–64.

14. R. I. Lissak and B. H. Sheppard, Beyond fairness: The criterion problem in research on dispute intervention, *Journal of Applied Social Psychology* 13 (1983), 45–65.

15. P. J. Carnevale and D. Conlon, Time pressure and mediator strategy

in a simulated organizational dispute, *Organizational Behavior and Human Decision Processes* 40 (1987), 111–33; D. Kressel and D. G. Pruitt, Themes in the mediation of social conflict, *Journal of Social Issues* 41 (1985), 179–98.

16. Carnevale and Conlon, Time pressure and mediator strategy.

17. R. Karambayya and J. M. Brett, Managers handling disputes: Third party roles and perceptions of fairness, *Academy of Management Journal* 32 (1989), 687–704.

18. F. A. Heller, *Managerial decision making: A study of leadership styles and power-sharing among senior executives* (London: Tavistock, 1971); F. A. Heller, *Competence and power in managerial decision making: A study of senior levels of organization in eight countries* (New York: John Wiley and Sons, 1981).

CHAPTER 16. Competitive Bidding: The Winner's Curse Revisited

1. D. Barry, Some people will watch—or eat—anything, *Chicago Tribune,* 1 April 1990, *Chicago Magazine,* pp. 41–2.

2. M. H. Bazerman and W. F. Samuelson, I won the auction but don't want the prize, *Journal of Conflict Resolution* 27 (1983), 618–34.

3. Ibid.

4. R. Thaler, The winner's curse, *The Journal of Economic Perspectives* 2 (1989), 191–202. Thaler used the term "penny aversion" in response to individuals not wanting to taking home hundreds of pennies.

5. Bazerman and Samuelson, I won the auction.

6. Ibid.

7. This analysis assumes that the commodity has a relatively fixed value across bidders; however, if you value the item more than the other bidders, you may purposefully bid higher to ensure winning the auction.

8. Bazerman and Samuelson, I won the auction.

9. D. Dyer, J. H. Kagel, and D. Levin, The winner's curse in low price auctions, unpublished manuscript, University of Houston, 1987.

10. E. C. Capen, R. V. Clapp, and W. M. Campbell, Competitive bidding in high risk situations, *Journal of Petroleum Technology* 23 (1971), 641–53.

11. W. Mead, A. Moseidjord, and P. Sorensen, The rate of return earned by lessees under cash bonus bidding of OCS oil and gas leases, *The Energy Journal* 4 (1983), 37–52.

12. To win a bidding war doesn't insure success of merged companies, *The Wall Street Journal,* September 1981, p. 1.

13. Rapaport, *Creating shareholder value.*
14. R. Dickie, A. Michel, and I. Shaked, The winner's curse in the merger game, *Journal of General Management* (Spring 1987), 32–51.
15. R. Roll, The hubris hypothesis of corporate takeovers, *Journal of Business* 59 (1986), 197–216.
16. J. P. Dessauer, *Book Publishing* (New York: Bowker, 1981).
17. J. Cassing, and R. W. Douglas, Implications of the auction mechanism in baseball's free agent draft, *Southern Economic Journal* 47 (July 1980), 110–21.
18. Dave Barry, personal communication, January 1991.

CHAPTER 17. Negotiation through Action

1. G. Hardin, The tragedy of the commons, *Science* 162 (1968), 1243–48.
2. Ibid.
3. Dawes, *Rational choice.*
4. A. Rapaport and A. M. Chammah, *Prisoner's Dilemma* (Ann Arbor: University of Michigan Press, 1965).
5. Dawes, *Rational choice.*
6. R. Axelrod, *The Evolution of Cooperation* (New York: Basic Books, 1984).
7. Trouble in paradise, *Newsweek,* 7 May 1990, p. 37.
8. T. C. Schelling, *Micromotives and macrobehaviors* (New York: W. W. Norton, 1978).
9. Dawes, *Rational choice.*
10. Ibid.
11. Ibid.

Index